Fantasy Cakes

Fantasy Cakes

Exciting new ideas for cake making and decorating

Lucy Poulton

David & Charles
Newton Abbot London

CIP data is available on request from the British Library

ISBN 0 7153 9812 1

First published in Australia
by Penguin Books Australia Ltd 1990

First published in Great Britain
by David & Charles 1990

Produced by Viking O'Neil
56 Claremont Street, South Yarra, Victoria 3141, Australia
a division of Penguin Books Australia Ltd

Printed in Hong Kong
by Bookbuilders Limited

for David & Charles Publishers plc
Brunel House Newton Abbot Devon

Contents

Conversion Tables

Weights

Metric	Imperial
15 g	½ oz
30 g	1 oz
60 g	2 oz
90 g	3 oz
125 g	4 oz
185 g	6 oz
250 g	8 oz
500 g	16 oz (1 lb)
1000 g (1 kg)	32 oz (2 lb)

Liquid Measures

Metric	Imperial	Household measure
5 ml	—	1 teaspoon
15 ml	½ fl oz	—
30 ml	1 fl oz	1 tablespoon
60 ml	3 fl oz	—
150 ml	5 fl oz	—
250 ml	8 fl oz	1 cup
600 ml	20 fl oz	1 pint

Cake Tin Sizes

Metric	Imperial
15 cm	6 in
17 cm	7 in
20 cm	8 in
22 cm	9 in
25 cm	10 in
30 cm	12 in

Oven Temperature Guide

	Electric		Gas	
	°C	°F	°C	°F
Low or cool	95	200	95	200
Very slow	120	250	120	250
Slow or warm	150	300	150–160	300–325
Moderately slow	160	325	160–175	325–350
Moderate	175	350	175–190	350–375
Moderately hot	190	375	190–205	375–400
Hot	205	400	205–230	400–450
Very hot	230	450	230–260	450–500

Introduction

Fantasy Cakes is a book for all cake decorators who want decorating to be creative and fun. Too often 'novelty' cakes – particularly those for children's parties – are boringly plain and unoriginal; too often they rely on lollies and hundreds and thousands, and not on genuinely novel effects, for their decoration.

Yet one of the great rewards of producing novelty cakes should be the delight and satisfaction that come from creating something truly original. *Fantasy Cakes* offers you designs that are new and unusual in themselves and also adaptable to your particular needs. Use the ideas in this book as the basis for your *own* creations.

Novelty cake decorating is fun as well as artistically satisfying. It does not demand the perfection required of the traditional floral wedding cake. Rather, it frees you to create fantasy and whimsy from a humble cake. And mistakes that would otherwise be considered a disaster can be turned to your advantage. Accidents can become great masterpieces!

Novelty cakes also have the advantage of being suitable for any occasion and for young and old alike. Men, in particular, often find novelty cakes more appropriate than traditional ones; and, of course, novelty cakes are the highlight of any festivity involving children.

Hopefully, *Fantasy Cakes* will not only bring excitement and cheer to your celebrations, but also put back the fun in your cake decorating and lead you to new adventures in sugar and cake.

Equipment

You will need various tools to produce the cakes presented in this book, and these are discussed in the following pages. The chapter is not, however, meant to provide a comprehensive list of equipment available for other, more general cake-decorating work. Remember that often, when you do not own a particular piece of equipment, you can successfully improvise with other items.

Icing Tubes

Star tubes numbers 5 or 8 were used for the shell edge of the Rainbow Cake and the World Map Cake. Writing tubes numbers 00, 0 and 1 were used for piping the various grass effects of the Miniature Garden Cake, and the number 1 tube was used to pipe the beading at the base of that cake. The Grass Trees were decorated with piped leaves, using a paper-cone bag cut to a V at its point.

Scissors

Use a large pair of scissors for general work and for cutting heavy wire. A small pair of embroidery scissors is very useful for cutting moulded items and smaller pieces, such as the clothes of the couple on the Cuddling Couch Cake.

Colours

Several types of food colourings were used for the cakes in the book: powdered food colouring, strong cake decorators' liquid colouring and paste colouring available from cake-decorating stores and some health food shops. In general, powdered food colouring is the easiest to use and provides a good, concentrated colour. When colouring large volumes of soft icing it is best to use small sachets of powdered food colouring or paste colours. Occasionally, petal dust makes an effective addition; it was used, for example, on the Ayers Rock Cake. Black food colouring is often not a true black, so petal dust can be used to help strengthen its colour. The subtle shades of petal dusts can often soften the tones of other food colourings and produce attractive mottled effects.

Paintbrushes

When selecting paintbrushes try to include one or two brushes that have a smooth, rounded tip to the handle, because this end is used frequently for moulding and frilling.

Round and flat sable brushes were used for most of the cakes in the book, but fine synthetic bristles can be a cheaper alternative. Select a 5 mm flat brush and numbers 0, 2, 4 and 6 round brushes. A thin, long-haired number 000 china-painting brush was used for the very fine line work on the World Map Cake.

Tweezers

Use tweezers to assist you when you are adding small, decorative pieces, such as the beads on the Face Masks, the tall spikes on the spinifex of the Ayers Rock Cake and the stamens on the Banksia Cones.

Parchmentene Paper-cone Bags

If parchmentene paper is not available, greaseproof or non-stick baking paper or tracing paper may be substituted, when you are making piping bags. A sheet of paper is cut into triangles, which are then rolled into small cones. The bags are filled with royal icing for piping work.

1 Fold a sheet of parchmentene paper into eight squares, as shown, then cut these into sixteen triangles.

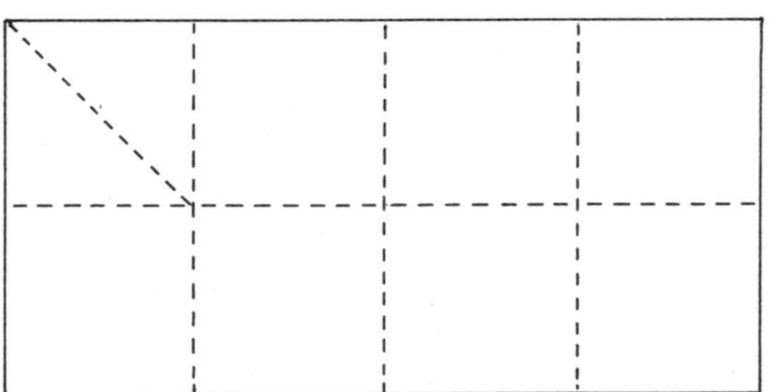

2 Take corner A of one triangle in your left hand and roll it forward to point X to form the beginning of a cone.

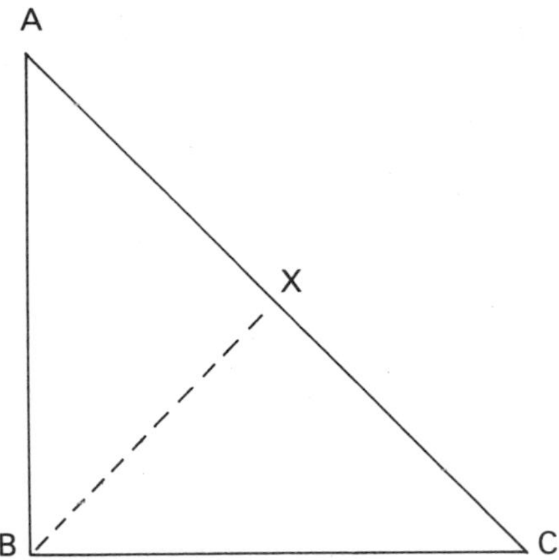

3 Wrap corner C around the partially formed cone to complete it. Ensure there is no hole at the base of the cone. The paper should overlap at the top of the cone at point B; make two inward folds there to secure the cone.

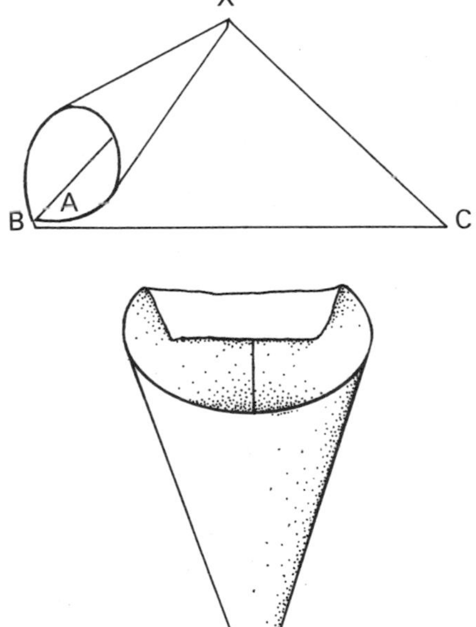

4 Half fill the bag with royal icing, fold the top inwards, cut a small hole at the point and, pressing on the flattened top, begin to pipe. When an icing tube needs to be inserted, cut away the paper 1–2 cm from the point of the cone and drop in the required tube, before proceeding to pipe.

Cutters

Cutters are often necessary to produce icing shapes. They can be bought or made from small strips of pliable metal such as empty soft-drink cans. Patterns of the cutters needed for particular cakes have been provided in the relevant chapters. After you have shaped the strips staple their ends together to hold the cutters in shape.

Stamens

A wide range of stamens can be bought from cake-decorating suppliers. Stamens with small heads were used for the tiny flowers on the Miniature Garden Cake and large, yellow-stemmed stamens were used on the Banksia Cones. Two-toned, bead-like stamens were used on the Face Masks and large white and red stamens created contrast on the Girls' Shoes.

Wire

Fairly thick wire was used as the central support for the necks of the Swans. Cotton-covered or silk-covered wire was used for the decorations of some of the other cakes; these wires are available from cake decorating stores. Silk-covered wire is used for very fragile icing flowers.

Rolling-pin

Use a large rolling-pin, about 500 mm long, for general rolling and covering work and a small, thin rolling-pin, about 150 mm long, for fine, small pieces.

Skewers

Thin bamboo skewers, such as those used for satays, are employed extensively as supports. They are also placed in the centre of shapes formed by combining two or more cakes.

Thicker, round-ended skewers are also used as modelling tools. A small cocktail stick can be employed for frilling and fluting icing pieces.

Art Knife or Scalpel

Use this to cut out small shapes that are difficult to go around with a pair of scissors.

Scrapers

Use cake scrapers to trim and smooth excess soft icing when you are covering cakes.

Spatula

A small, fine spatula is very handy for novelty cake decorating. Because it is very pliable it can be used to shape, mould and press the icing when other larger tools, such as regular cake scrapers, cannot do the job.

Garlic Crusher

A garlic crusher can be used in place of an extruder to create long strands of icing required for details, such as hair and blades of grass.

Decorating Tools

Decorators often have favourite tools that they have gathered over the years and find very versatile. Experiment a little with items in your home, especially if you do not wish to purchase a large collection of tools. However, you will find five wooden potters' tools and six cake decorators' tools, sold in kit form at most cake-decorating stores, particularly useful. Because a decorating tool is often known by many names, the tools are numbered not named in the following discussion.

Pottery Tools

Number 1 Its long, knife-like shape makes this tool handy for moulding creases, such as those given to the Bark Huts, the Rustic Boots and the Ayers Rock Cake. It is also very useful for flattening the terraces and steps of the Miniature Garden Cake and the Castle Cake.

Number 2 The ball at one end of this tool is handy for making large eye sockets and eyes. It was used for the eyes of the Dragon Cake and those of the Face Masks, and for smoothing the icing of the Beer Stein Cake at its base and on the underside of its lid.

The smooth, curved end was used extensively to create the contours of the Ayers Rock Cake and the veins on the wings of the Dragon Cake.

Number 3 The spoon-like shape at one end was used to mould the seed pockets of the Banksia Cones.

The flat, serrated end was used to create the corrugated iron effect in the icing of the roofs of the Bark Huts.

Number 4 The hooked end was useful for moulding the necks and heads of the animals on the Noah's Ark Cake.

The flat, curved end was used on the Dragon Cake, the Castle Cake and the Baobab Tree Cake.

Number 5 This doubly curved smoothing tool was used to make most of the creases and folds on the cakes that required them. One end is slightly more pointed than the other.

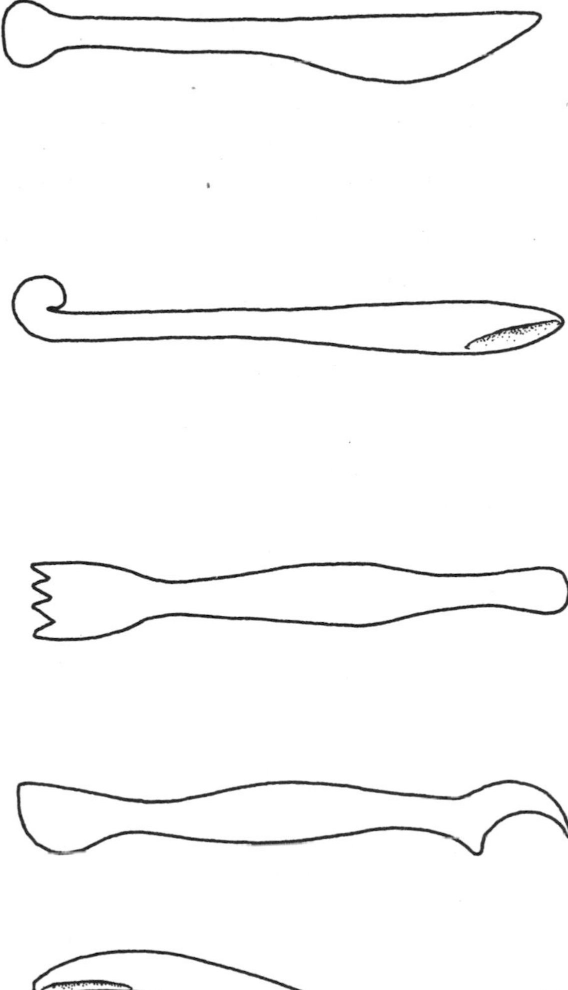

Cake Decorators' Tools

Number 1 This is another double-curved tool; however, the ends of this tool are more rounded. Bends and curves on the logs of the Bark Huts were created with this tool.

Number 2 This, with a ball at either end, is useful for shaping many flowers and all eye features.

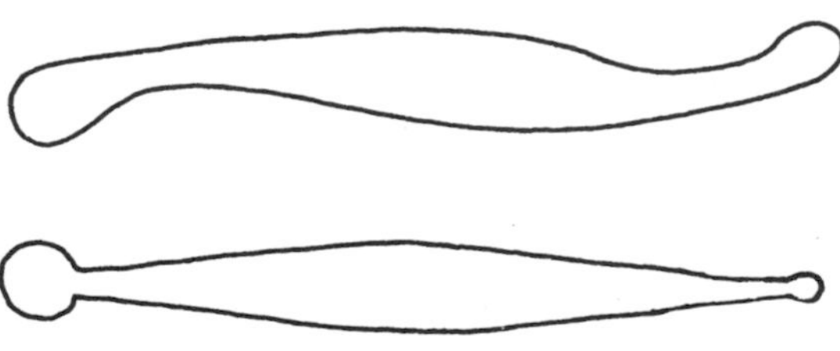

Number 3 The flat V-shape of this tool was handy for moulding small, tight areas, such as the nooks and crannies of the Castle Cake.

The lined, serrated and spoon-like shape of the other end is useful for marking webbed feet on animals. It was employed in the work on the Bark Huts.

Number 4 One end of this tool is a smooth cone, the other an umbrella shape. The smooth end is most effective for hollowing pieces of icing to a point and is used extensively for flowers. The ridged end is ideal for creating the dividing lines inside cup-shaped flowers.

Number 5 This tool has a short scoop at one end used to form eyes, creases and depressions, such as those pressed into the white decorative icing on the Beer Stein Cake.

The flat, serrated end is similar to that of the number 3 pottery tool.

Number 6 A long-handled needle is very handy for inserting items that are difficult to position with your fingers.

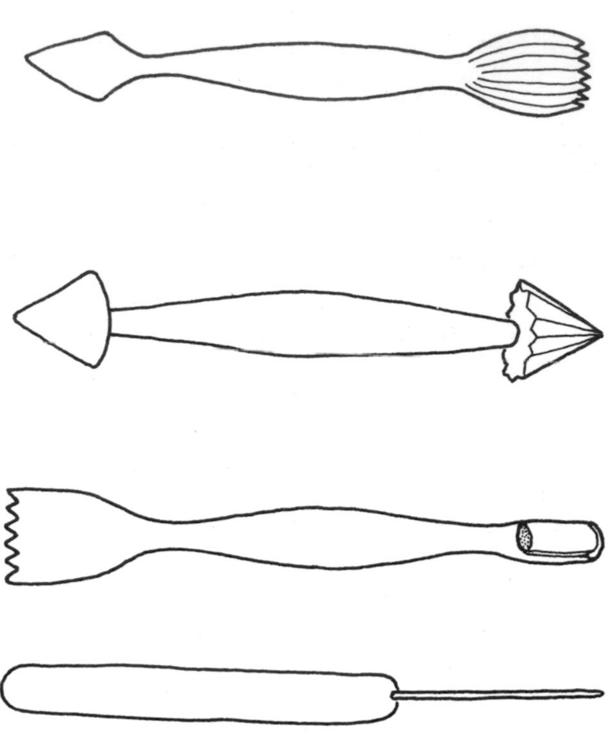

Cake Tins

The experimenting associated with novelty work extends to cake tins. As you will see from the instructions for a number of the cakes in the book, cooking moulds often have to be shaped from foil trays and containers. Unusual cake shapes in the book have also often been achieved by combining two or more cakes. Experiment with containers you find at home, such as casseroles, pie dishes or garden pots, to create exciting shapes for your fantasy cakes.

Items such as a ruler, a tape measure, aluminium foil, fine plastic film, a small, clean comb, spoons, knives, professional cake slides, a turntable, cotton wool and cotton wool buds are useful from time to time, but not essential.

Recipes

Cakes

All the cakes produced for this book were made from the Basic Fruit Cake mixture, given below. However, wherever indicated throughout the book, alternative types of cake may be used, so this chapter includes a selection of suitable recipes. The amount of cake mixture required by each cake in the book is noted at the start of the chapters.

Unless otherwise stated, the recipes in this chapter are for 20-cm cakes. It is possible to make larger or smaller cakes by varying the quantities of the ingredients, though the ratio of one ingredient to another should always remain constant. The size of a cake is determined by the amount of butter used. The Basic Fruit Cake, which requires a 20-cm baking tin, uses 250 g of butter. The following table is a guide to the size of tin required for different volumes of cake mixture, according to weight of butter.

Cake Mixture	Size of Tin
125 g butter	15 cm
250 g butter	20 cm
500 g butter	25 cm
750 g butter	30 cm

To assess the quantity of cake mixture required for a novelty tin or an aluminium foil mould, fill a regular 20-cm tin with water to the usual height for a 20-cm mixture (that is, to about 2 cm from the top). Pour the water into a measuring jug and use it as a guide. Novelty tins or aluminium foil moulds may take, for example, half or double the water: increase or decrease the quantity of cake mixture accordingly. Note that baking times will vary if the recipe is changed.

All the following recipes require an oven preheated to the baking temperature specified, unless otherwise indicated.

Basic Fruit Cake

250 g raisins
250 g currants
125 g mixed peel
125 g glacé cherries
500 g sultanas
125 g blanched almonds, chopped
½ cup rum, brandy or sherry
1 tablespoon glycerine
250 g butter
250 g sugar
1 tablespoon marmalade
5 eggs, beaten
250 g plain flour
60 g self-raising flour
pinch salt
1 teaspoon ground nutmeg
1 teaspoon mixed, ground spice

Preheat oven to 180°C.

Chop all the large fruits and the nuts. Place all the fruits and nuts in a bowl and then pour over them the rum, brandy or sherry and glycerine and allow to stand for a minimum of 24 hours. If a richer flavour is required, more of the liquor may be used and the mixture can be allowed to stand for up to a month. Stir the fruit daily and keep the bowl well covered to avoid evaporation of the liquid.

Sift the dry ingredients together. Mix the cake with your hands to avoid damaging the fruit, which can happen if you use a mixing machine. The warmth of your body will also assist even creaming.

Cream the butter and sugar together. Add the marmalade and keep working the mixture.

Gradually add the previously beaten eggs, making sure to add just a little egg at a time and to mix thoroughly between each addition.

If the mixture curdles at this point, add a little sifted flour after each addition of egg. This will ensure the fruit is evenly distributed when the cake is baked.

Add half the fruit, mixing it in well, then the remaining flour and spices and the last of the fruit. Stir the mixture thoroughly. Place it in a greased and floured cake tin or aluminium foil mould.

Dip a soup spoon into a glass of hot water, then smooth down the top of the cake with it. Repeat this until the surface has been smoothed and a very fine film of water has formed all over the top of the cake.

Place a piece of aluminium foil over the top of the tin or mould and put the tin or mould on a baking tray. Lower the oven temperature to 140°C and bake the cake slowly for 3–4 hours.

When the cake is cooked, remove it from the oven. Leave it in its tin or mould, covered with a thick towel, for 24 hours so that the steam will condense and return to the cake, ensuring a moist, rich fruit cake.

The following cake recipes are offered as alternatives, if you wish to use a mixture other than the traditional fruit cake one. Unless otherwise instructed, mix the cakes and bake them at the same temperature as specified in the Basic Fruit Cake recipe.

Tropical Delight Fruit Cake

500 g dried or glacé pineapple
500 g dried apricots
125 g glacé cherries
60 g glacé orange
60 g glacé peaches
60 g hazelnuts, chopped
1 cup brandy
250 g butter
250 g sugar
1 tablespoon plum and peach jam
5 eggs, beaten
200 g plain flour
60 g self-raising flour
1 cup dessicated coconut

Allow the fruit to stand in the brandy for a minimum of 3 days.

Bake for 3–4 hours.

This cake has a wonderful, rich range of pale colours, highlighted by the red of the glacé cherries.

Banana Cake

270 g self-raising flour
120 g sugar
2 eggs, beaten
4 medium-sized, ripe bananas
2 teaspoons cinnamon
⅓ cup oil

Beat all the ingredients together until light and fluffy. Pour into a well-greased tin.

Bake at 200°C for approximately 45 minutes.

Coconut Cake

120 g butter or margarine
180 g sugar
90 g dessicated coconut
2 eggs
180 g self-raising flour
3 tablespoons powdered milk
½ cup water

Cream the butter or margarine and sugar together. Add the dessicated coconut, then the eggs one at a time. Mix in the self-raising flour and the powdered milk. Finally add the water gradually. Beat the mixture until it is rich and creamy.

Bake the cake at 200°C for approximately 40 minutes.

Sultana and Cherry Cake

180 g butter or margarine
240 g sugar
3 eggs
180 g self-raising flour
180 g plain flour
⅔ cup milk

180 g sultanas
180 g glacé cherries

Cream the butter and sugar together until light and fluffy. Add the eggs one by one, beating the mixture well each time, then the self-raising and plain flours and the milk. Beat the mixture until it is creamy. Finally add the sultanas and glacé cherries. The mixture is best baked in a well-greased 22-cm or 25-cm tin. If the cake needs to be very high use a smaller tin.

Bake the cake at 200°C for approximately 60 minutes.

Marsala Cake

A rich Marsala cake can be made by using the Sultana and Cherry Cake recipe (above), but omitting the sultanas and the glacé cherries and adding 60 ml of Marsala. Use vanilla-flavoured sugar for this cake to add more flavour.

Chocolate Hazelnut Cake

4 eggs, separated
120 g sugar
1 tablespoon honey
60 g self-raising flour
100 g cornflour
1 teaspoon cream of tartar
½ teaspoon bicarbonate of soda
1 teaspoon cinnamon
¾ cup chocolate cake or chocolate biscuit crumbs
½ cup ground hazelnuts

Whip the egg yolks until they are almost white and creamy. Add the sugar and whip again. Stir in the honey. Fold in the self-raising flour, cornflour, cream of tartar, bicarbonate of soda and cinnamon. Beat the mixture well so that it remains light and fluffy. In another bowl whip the egg whites until they are also light and fluffy, then fold in the cake or biscuit crumbs and hazelnuts. Fold the two mixtures together and pour into a 25-cm tin.

Bake the cake at 200°C for approximately 25–35 minutes.

Although this cake is quite light, it is suitable for novelty work as long as the icing required is not thick.

Carrot Cake

5 eggs, separated
180 g sugar
400 g carrot, finely grated
350 g almonds, finely ground
few drops almond essence
90 g self-raising flour

Whip the egg yolks until they are white and creamy. Add the sugar, then beat again. Whip the egg whites in another bowl until they are stiff. Add the whites, grated carrot and the ground almonds to the egg yolk mixture. Fold in the self-raising flour and add the almond essence. Pour the mixture into a well-greased tin.

Bake at 200°C for approximately 50 minutes.

Icings

The quantity of icing required will vary according to the size of the cake. Use the following chart as a guide.

Size of Cake	Quantity of Icing
15 cm	500–750 g
20 cm	1 kg
25 cm	1.5 kg
30 cm	2 kg

A fruit cake requires equal quantities of almond icing and soft icing. A little more almond or soft icing will usually be required for patching any holes or cracks in the cake.

Soft Icing

This icing is also known as sugar paste, fondant or plastic icing, according to the manufacturer. No recipe is included for it because it is readily available in stores, and the bought icing is often more reliable in its consistency than the home-made. Soft icing is rolled out with a rolling-pin in the same manner as pastry and is used in a similar way.

Marzipan

Marzipan is also usually purchased. It is made predominantly from almonds and sugar, and the oil of the almonds makes it very pliant and therefore a suitable (and inexpensive) substitute for soft or almond icing.

Almond Icing

Again, no recipe is given because the shop-bought icing has a better consistency than the home-made.

Butter Icing

125 g butter
500 g icing sugar
10 ml vanilla essence
125 ml water, juice or milk

Cream the butter and sugar together. Add the vanilla essence. Stir in the water, juice or milk, a little at a time until you have the required consistency. It may not be necessary to add all the liquid.

Royal Icing

Royal icing is used for piped embroidery, lace, extension work, flowers and shell borders.

The consistency of royal icing is adjusted according to its intended use. It should be soft and free flowing for fine line work, and much firmer for flowers or shell borders so that it holds the particular shape.

Royal icing will keep in the refrigerator for 2–6 weeks. It is best, however, to make a fresh quantity each time you need it, if possible, or at least to remove any dry icing from the top and mix the icing again to return some body to it.

1 egg white
250 g pure icing sugar
lemon juice, if required

If flowers are to be piped, it is often not necessary to sift the sugar. On the other hand, if fine extension work is intended, it is necessary to sift the sugar 3–4 times. Use a fine piece of silk or a very fine gauge sifter. It is now possible to buy superfine, pure icing sugar that does not require sifting if it is used while it is still fresh.

Sift the icing sugar, if required. Break the egg white with a fork, then add it to the sugar and mix well. Stir until the mixture looks smooth and very white. Add lemon juice, if softer icing is required. Place a fine film of plastic on the surface of the icing to stop a skin from forming. Note that this should be left on the icing at all times, otherwise the hard skin that forms will block the tip of fine tubes.

If a particularly fluffy and smooth icing is required, whip the egg white first, then add the icing sugar gradually, making sure you mix the icing well after each addition.

Soft-peak, Medium-peak and Firm-peak Royal Icings

The consistency of royal icing (see preceding recipe) is varied by increasing or reducing the amount of liquid added to the icing sugar. If just a little extra liquid is required, a squeeze of lemon juice will suffice. However, if the mixture is very dry and will not hold together, another egg white will be required. Note that whites in eggs of the same size vary in volume throughout the year, so adjustments need to be made accordingly.

To test that royal icing is at the soft-peak stage draw the icing up to a peak with a knife. The peak should begin to collapse immediately, but should not disappear altogether. Firm-peak icing will retain a stiff peak. Medium-peak icing represents a stage between soft- and firm-peak icing.

Gum Paste

1 tablespoon gelatine
1 teaspoon cream of tartar
½ cup water
500 g pure icing sugar
1 cup cornflour

Place the first three ingredients in a saucepan and warm for a short time to dissolve the

Easy Gift Cake

(see page 23)

Castle Cake

(see page 27)

gelatine. The mixture should be no more than lukewarm to the touch otherwise the gelatine's glutinous properties will be destroyed.

Add the dry ingredients and stir well. Place a damp cloth over the mixture and allow the paste to cool for an hour. Remove the cloth and stir once again. Pack the paste into small containers and store in the freezer. Remove a container from the freezer when needed; the paste does not require time to thaw. The mixture will keep for a minimum of 6 months in the freezer.

Do not use until 24 hours have elapsed after making. Add cornflour to small pieces of paste until a nice, firm mixture has been worked up. The amount of cornflour required varies but the paste is ready when it feels like Plasticine and turns white. When it is ready, place it in a plastic bag to prevent it from drying out. Note that the paste dries out very fast in hot conditions. If your hands are hot, cool them occasionally in cold water to reduce the problem of the paste drying out. Dried-out pieces of paste cannot be re-used, so it is best to discard them.

If considerable elasticity is required, increase the quantity of gelatine to up to double the amount given in the recipe.

Piping Jelly

This recipe may be used if you have difficulty purchasing piping jelly, although it does not have a very long lifespan.

¼ cup lemon juice
1 level tablespoon cornflour
¼ cup water
4 tablespoons castor sugar

Place all the ingredients in a small saucepan and dissolve them over a low heat. Stir continuously until the mixture comes to the boil. Allow it to thicken, then remove it from the heat. If the mixture thickens too much, add a little more water. Colour as required with liquid food colours. Store in the refrigerator.

Covering the Cake

The shapes of novelty cakes are formed by a combination of the cake's shape, built-up areas of icing and various moulded pieces of soft icing added to the cake.

Traditional decorated cakes use a fruit cake as their basis. They are covered first with a layer of almond icing, then with one of soft icing. The cakes are treated in this way for two reasons: to seal the cake; and to prevent the outer covering from being spoiled by fruit stains. Novelty cakes, on the other hand, do not take as long to produce and their icing is usually brighter and so less likely to show stains. Therefore the strict icing requirements of the traditional cake are not quite so important. The type and number of coverings will depend on the cake recipe used and the visual effects required.

Because all the cakes produced for this book were made from a fruit mixture, they, with few exceptions, received two coverings. However, where it is indicated that other recipes may be used, the cakes may be covered with only one layer of icing, and it does not always have to be the traditional soft icing. Alternative coverings are suggested throughout the book where they are appropriate. But, because soft icing (and almond icing) is very pliable and elastic, it makes the ideal medium for moulded decorative effects.

In fact, it is possible to press and mould soft icing onto and over any shape and size of cake. The only requirements are that the icing be rolled out to a size large enough to cover the entire cake and that it be smoothed into and over all the various bends and curves. A slightly thicker than normal covering of soft icing will ensure that the final surface is smooth.

The amount of soft icing required for each of the cakes in the book is given at the beginning of the chapter. If a first covering of almond icing is also used, buy the amount specified for soft icing. When an alternative to soft icing is indicated, the quantity will vary according to the thickness required to achieve the desired effect.

Almond Icing Covering

1 Place your cake right side up on a working board. Knead some bought almond icing with your hands to warm and soften it, then press small pieces into any holes in the cake. Also patch any parts of the cake where pieces are missing. Build up areas of almond icing to rectify any unevenness in the cake's shape. If two or more cakes are being joined together, fill the spaces between them with almond icing.

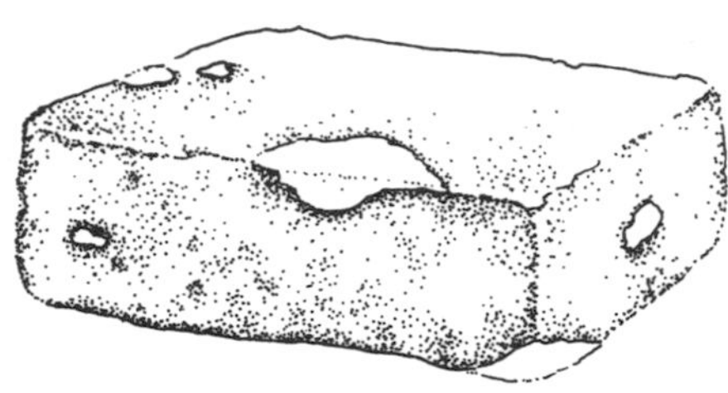

2 When making novelty cakes it is important to cover your cake on the presentation board. Scrape a little royal icing (see Recipes chapter) onto the base of the cake, then attach it to the board.

3 Glaze all the cake surfaces with some warmed apricot jam. Knead then roll out enough almond icing to cover the entire cake. Turn the board so that the cake's length runs from left to right.

4 Place a rolling-pin across the part of the rolled-out icing farthest from you, roll one-third of the icing onto it with a forward motion and allow the remainder to hang down.

Place the icing on the rolling-pin in front of the cake so that the piece hanging down just touches the base of the board on the side closest to you. Also ensure that the icing is equidistant from the left and right sides of the cake to ensure that it will cover the cake evenly. Unroll the icing, allowing it to fall across the top of the cake and down the rear side.

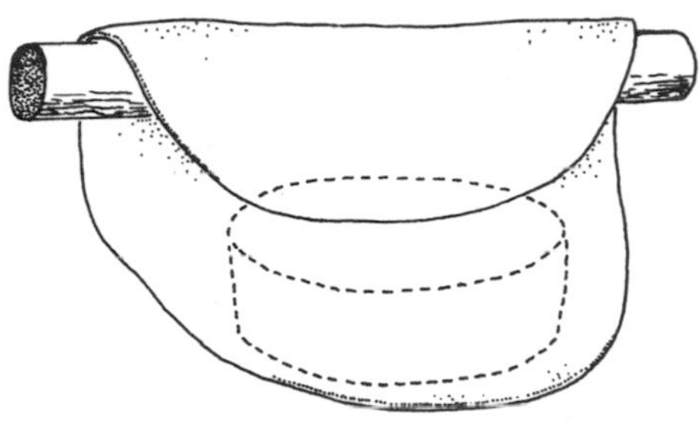

5 Slowly but systematically press down on the top rim of the cake with your hands. If there are any folds and creases in the icing on the sides of the cake use one hand to pull the icing out and away from the cake, then the other to press the icing back against the side. Work in this way all around the cake, gradually progressing down the sides until all the icing has been pressed and smoothed. In this way all the folds and creases are moved away from the cake, down onto the excess icing beyond the cake's base.

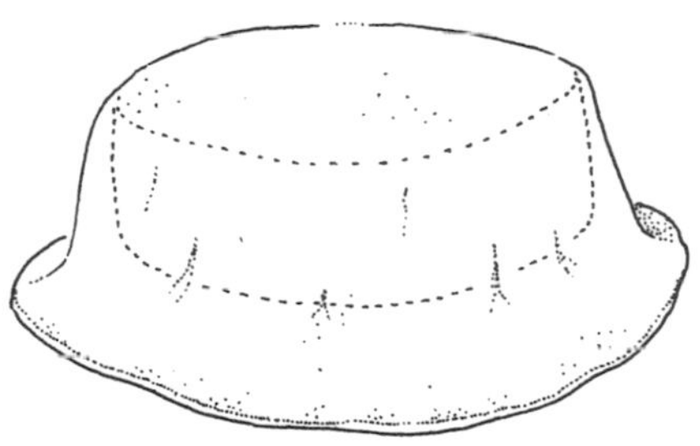

6 Use your hands to press and smooth the icing gently on the top and sides of the cake. If the cake is an unusual shape, air pockets may occur; these will need to be removed before the icing can fit snugly over all the surface. Use a fine pin to prick the air bubbles, then press gently around the area to help release the air.

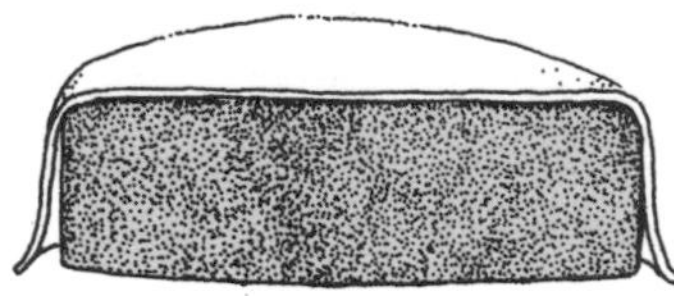

7 Press and smooth the sides of the cake, then use a scraper or sharp knife to trim the icing, so that a 1–2-cm border of excess icing remains. Push the icing at the base against the cake's sides to expel any trapped air.

8 Cut away the remaining excess icing. This should be done in small sections at a time. Press the cut edge against the base as you progress around the cake. Use scrapers or a spatula to smooth and neaten the base edge.

9 Allow the icing to dry thoroughly before covering it with a second layer of icing: sometimes a week will be required. During this time store the cake in a cupboard or box, but never under plastic or in the refrigerator. Air must be able to circulate around the cake at all times.

Soft Icing Covering

1 The next covering – one of soft icing – is applied in exactly the same way as the one of almond icing. Glaze the almond icing with egg white before adding the layer of soft icing.

When making novelty cakes it is usual to colour the soft icing before applying it to the cake. Final touches of colour can be added after the cake has been covered and decorated.

2 Allow the icing to become firm before decorating further or using (see Step 9 for Almond Icing Covering, above).

See colour plate

on page 17

Easy Gift Cake

The Easy Gift Cake is a quick and straightforward cake that can be made when you require a cake instantly. Any of the cake recipes listed in the Recipes chapter are suitable so the time and cost involved in making a fruit cake need not be a deterrent to you trying the Easy Gift Cake.

The icing on the cake looks like paper wrapping around a gift. The cake will actually be more attractive if the icing is not absolutely flat and flawless – good news for those who find it difficult to cover a cake smoothly! Note, though, that it is only possible to achieve a wrapped effect with an icing that can be rolled out like pastry.

The decorations are printed on the icing, using one or several potato stamps. The patterns can be varied according to the celebration. The final touch is a purchased multi-looped bow and a matching ribbon tied around the cake. These can be varied in size and colour to suit the theme of the pattern.

The cake illustrated required one quantity of cake mixture (250 g butter) and 1 kg of bought soft icing.

Potato Stamps

Patterns can be traced from pictures or designs or cut out freehand.

1 Select several potatoes of different sizes. Use an art knife or scalpel to cut each potato through the middle at its thickest part so that the two cut faces are a good size. If a chosen pattern is drawn or traced, place it on a cut face and then cut around its outline with a knife or blade. A freehand design can be cut straight into the face. Ensure the cut is at least 4 mm deep.

Use a sharp knife to remove the flesh around the design so that the pattern is raised. Take care that you do not accidently remove any section of the design. Cut again around any areas that are not sharp and clear. The following patterns were used for decorating the cake shown in the colour plate.

2 Wipe the potato stamps with a paper towel, then place them on another sheet of dry paper while the cake is covered.

Covering the Cake

1 Bake a cake in any geometric shape or size. Allow it to cool, then remove it from its tin.

2 If the cake selected is a fruit one, fill and patch any holes or depressions with bought almond or soft icing before glazing it. Glaze the whole cake with a little warmed apricot jam. If you are using a fruit cake, cover it with a thin layer of bought almond icing (see the chapter on Covering the Cake). A layer of almond icing is only required, however, for fruit cakes that are not to be used immediately. If the cake is to be used within the week, or if it is a soft cake, only soft icing is necessary.

3 Select a presentation board that will complement the size, shape and colour scheme of the cake. Use two broad cake slides (professional catering ones are strongest) to place the cake on the board. It is best to scrape a little royal icing (see Recipes chapter) on the board beforehand, to which the cake can adhere. If you have added an almond icing covering, there is no need to wait for it to become firm before applying its final covering, but it must be glazed with egg white before you add the soft icing.

4 Take a quantity of soft icing appropriate to the size of the cake chosen (see Recipes chapter). The icing will be most effective if left white or only coloured in a pale shade.

To colour the soft icing take a small ball of icing and add a drop or two of your selected colour. Knead the ball well, then knead it into the larger quantity of icing thoroughly. Roll the icing into a large ball. Cut through it to test for evenness of colour: if no marbling shows, the icing is ready to use; if streaks show, knead the icing again and repeat the testing process.

5 Measure the cake from the base of one of its long sides, across its top and down to the base of its other long side. Roll out the icing thinly to a rectangle. The width of the rectangle should be the same as the measurement taken from the cake and no wider. The length of the rectangle should be a little longer than that of the cake.

6 Place the icing on the cake as described in the chapter on Covering the Cake. Gently press the edges of the top so that the icing adheres to the cake. Use a scraper to smooth and ease the icing on the two long sides of the cake and to trim off any excess at the bases. Gently rub the top of the cake to smooth it down, also. Do not yet work icing overhanging or extending beyond the short sides of the cake.

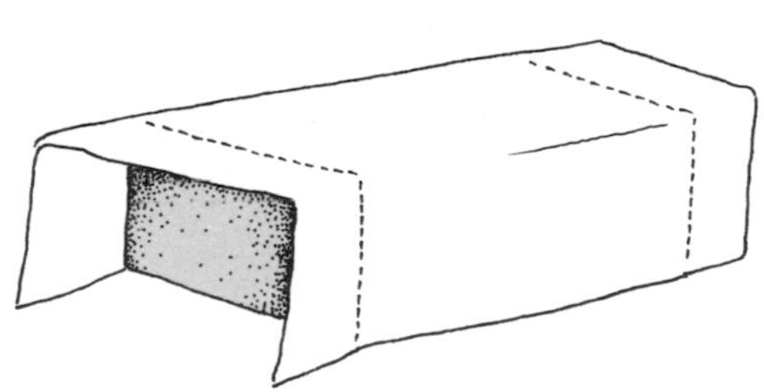

7 Roll out two small, rectangular pieces of icing and place them on the short sides of the cake, at the centre base of the cake. Smooth them gently with your fingers.

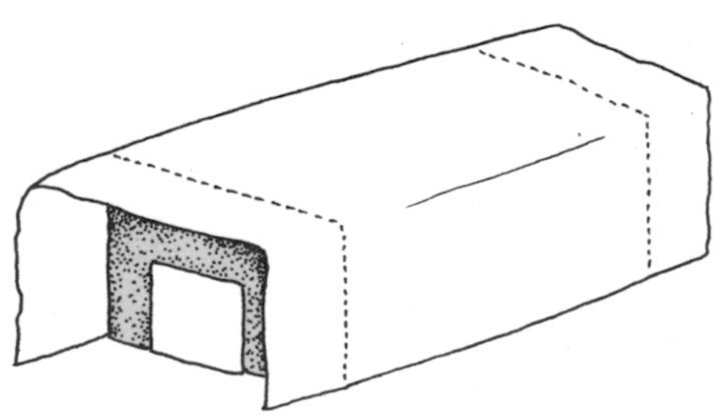

8 Press the icing overhanging the top of the cake down one short side to meet the top of the rectangle of icing. The two edges should just meet: use a pair of scissors to cut away any excess. Repeat the procedure for the other short side.

9 Bring the two flaps of icing that extend beyond one of the short sides in towards the centre of that side, tucking under the tops of the flaps to form nice, crisp, diagonal fold lines as you do so. Repeat the procedure for the other side. If the joins and folds are too bulky they can be pressed down a little with the aid of a scraper. However, take care not to destroy the effect of layers of wrapped paper.

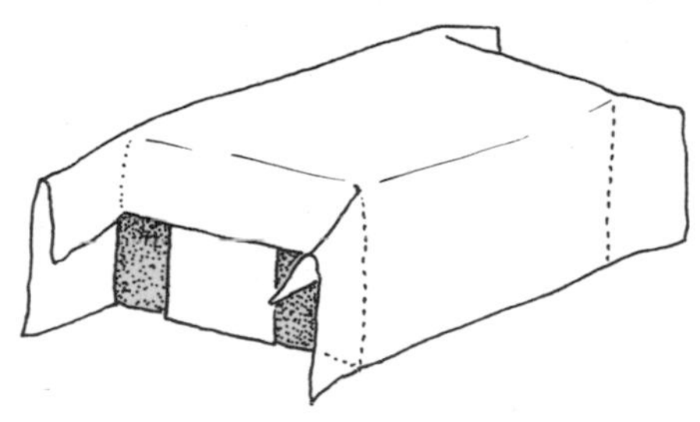

10 Smooth any areas that you think need it, using your hands and scrapers. For best results, set the cake aside to dry before adding the pattern. However, if no spare time is available, you can print on the icing while it is still soft.

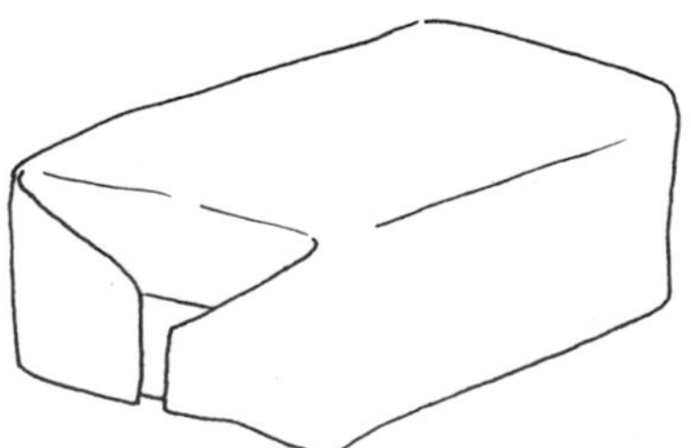

Printing the Pattern

1 Select paste colours because they will not run and smear as easily as other forms of colouring. Brush a good coat of colour on all sections of the potato stamps with a paintbrush, but do not be too generous. Practise using the potato stamps, by pressing them onto a spare piece of rolled-out icing, until you feel happy that you can use them without smudging the icing. The sections of each potato stamp can be coloured the same or differently.

2 When all the stamps have been coloured, print the pattern on the cake covering. Be sure to intersperse the different motifs to create a pleasing effect. If there are any smudges or excess spots of colour rub these gently with a cotton bud. The cotton bud will absorb extra colour, ensuring the pattern dries evenly.

3 Once the pattern has been completed, use a food Texta colour or a fine brush to draw or paint fine details, such as those shown in the colour plate. The balloon strings and party-hat streamers were painted on with a fine brush.

4 Set the cake aside to dry for a while before adding the ribbon.

5 Approximately 1.5 m of ribbon were required for the cake illustrated. The ribbon used was a red, fancy-edged paper ribbon. Take a length of the ribbon and gently ease one end under the cake on one side, pull the ribbon up over the cake top and down the other side and push its remaining end under the cake. A small spatula is useful for pushing the ends under, and scrapings of royal icing underneath the cake will hold the ribbon ends in place, if need be. Repeat the procedure for the other two sides of the cake, using another length of the ribbon. The two lengths of ribbon should cross each other somewhere on the top of the cake. Place a purchased multi-looped bow on top of the cake where the ribbons meet. Cut the remaining ribbon in two to form the tails and slide these into place under the bow.

See colour plate on page 18

Castle Cake

Castles are a source of great delight for young and old alike. As youngsters we are enthralled by mystery tales of castles, dungeons and misty moors. These fantasies change as we grow older. For some, castles represent travel and wealth; for others, peace and ownership, since it is often said that your home is your castle, implying a castle is a place where you can indulge yourself and enjoy a hard-earned rest. Consequently, the Castle Cake should appeal to both sexes and to all age groups.

Instructions are given for reproducing the cake illustrated; however, the castle can be made larger or smaller depending on your needs. For small celebrations fewer turrets can be included, so less cake mixture will be required; the reverse is applicable to a larger party. A children's cake, for example, might be larger, so that all guests can receive their own turret.

The instructions given are for fruit cakes covered with bought almond and soft icings. However, for children it may be desirable to substitute other varieties of cake and icing. But note that fruit cakes are better for achieving heights than softer cakes, which sink and collapse.

The cake illustrated required one to two quantities of cake mixture (250–500 g butter) and 2.5–3 kg of soft icing.

Shaping the Cake

The Castle Cake shown in the colour plate consists of: a rectangular main building; a much smaller, inner second storey; and seven towers and turrets, two of which (numbers 4 and 7) include smaller, upper towers (numbers 5 and 8). When viewed from the back (see photograph) the castle can be seen to include an open courtyard, the walls of which link two turrets (numbers 1 and 2) to the main building. These outlying turrets may be deleted or increased in number according to your needs.

Back of castle

1 For the Castle Cake illustrated you will need to bake the number and type of cakes given in the following table.

Castle Part	Cake Tin	Height	Diameter
main building	20 cm rectangular		
first floor	made from cake cut away from main building		
turrets 1, 2, 7	cylindrical	9 cm	7 cm
turrets 3, 5	cylindrical	6 cm	7 cm
turrets 4, 9	cylindrical	13 cm	9 cm
turret 6	cylindrical	4–5 cm	7 cm

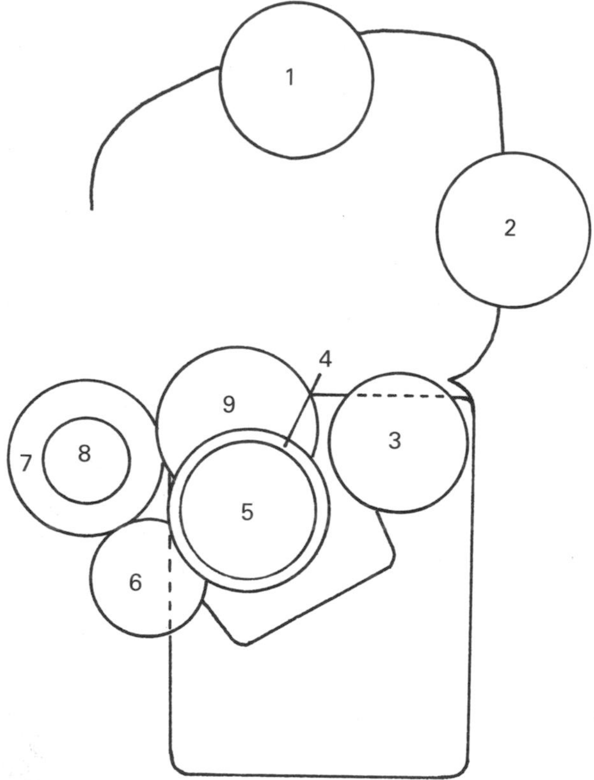

Ground-plan of castle

Note that turret number 8, on top of tower number 7, is made from icing, not cake, and that two small towers (numbers 3 and 6) do not start at ground level, but instead are suspended from the sides of the main building.

To achieve the different heights given for the turrets, which give the castle interest, vary the quantity of mixture you place in your cylindrical tins. It is not necessary to line the cylindrical tins. Oil the inside of each and then sprinkle in some plain flour. Allow the flour to coat all the sides and the bases, so that the cakes can be easily removed after baking.

Select a presentation board that is suitable for the number of cakes included. In the case of the Castle Cake illustrated, a large, oval board was used.

2 When the cakes are cool remove them from their tins. You can now commence building up the castle.

Cut away a section from the rectangular cake so that one of the turrets can fit in place. The piece removed is cut to shape and added to the main building as a small second storey.

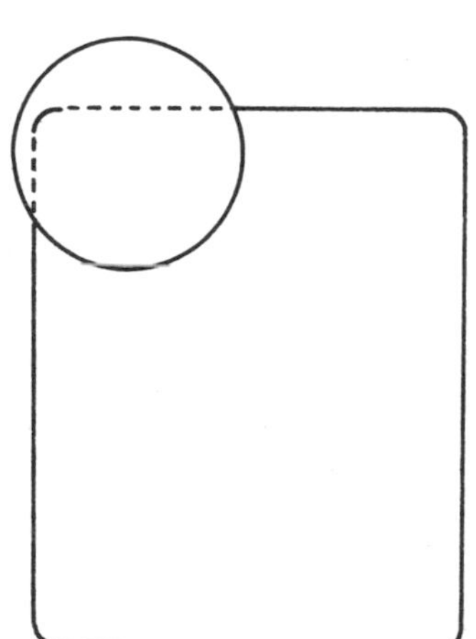

3 Fill in any holes or spaces in the cakes, using some bought almond icing. Scrape a little royal icing (see Recipes chapter) under the rectangular cake, the second storey and the turrets that are attached to the main building (but not turrets numbers 1 and 2 in the courtyard wall), and assemble the castle on the board, as shown in the ground-plan.

Covering the Cake

1 Glaze all the cakes with a little warmed apricot jam, then cover them with almond icing (see the chapter on Covering the Cake). You will probably find it easier to cover the cakes in sections; the joins will not be visible on the finished castle. Cover the two outlying towers (numbers 1 and 2) by rolling them along strips of icing.

2 Use soft icing to build the small turret (number 8) on top of tower number 7 and the spires on top of turrets numbers 1, 2, 3, 5, 6, 8 and 9. The colour plate shows an additional sugar spire slipped in behind turret number 6 and between turrets numbers 4 and 7 to fill a gap.

3 Set the castle aside to dry thoroughly before commencing on the final covering.

4 Glaze all the cakes with egg white, then cover them with a thin layer of soft icing that has been coloured. In the example a greyish beige was chosen. If there are joins in the icing, merge their edges by rubbing them gently with your hands; the warmth will make the lines disappear. The two unattached turrets (numbers 1 and 2) are added to the board once they have been rolled in oblongs of soft icing: scrape some royal icing under each and press them into place.

5 Colour some soft icing for the roofs of the spires either mauve or blue-mauve. Roll out small portions and, using the patterns below, which are to scale for the Castle Cake illustrated, cut out a number of triangular sections. Use the larger triangles for the larger spires. Up to nine triangles will be required for each spire.

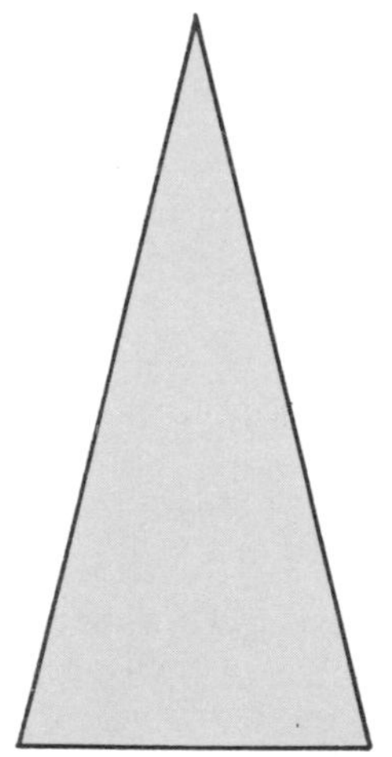

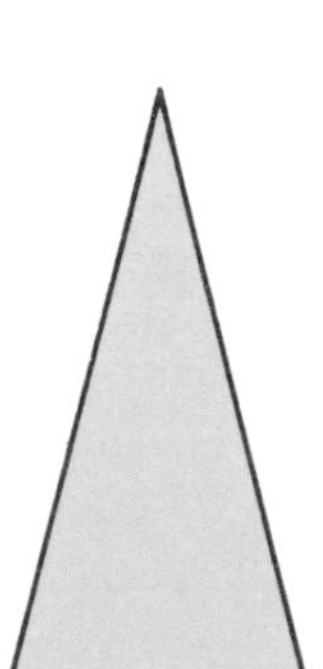

6 Moisten the bases of the triangles with a little water, then place them around the sugar spires, overlapping each triangle by about a third.

7 Use a pottery tool, such as the number 1 tool described in the Equipment chapter, to accentuate the lines of the joins. Pinch and squeeze the tips of the spires to give them a slightly pointed look at the top.

8 Use the same tool to make indentations in the icing for windows. Vary the windows in size for interest.

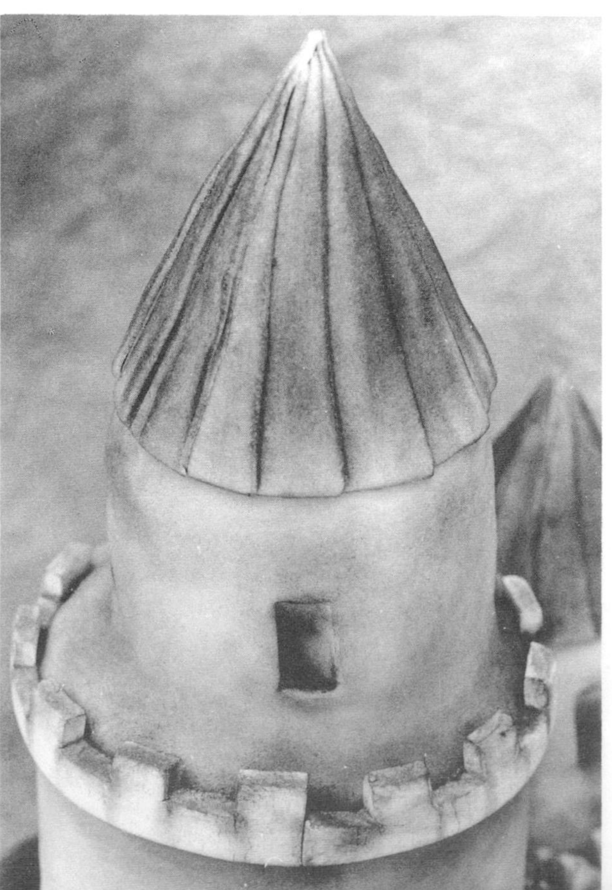

Walls and Parapets

Walls and parapets are very important because they greatly enhance the fortified appearance of the castle.

1 Gather all the leftover icing together and roll some of it into a thick, rectangular shape. Measure the distance between the rectangular cake and the first outlying turret (number 2). Cut a piece of the rolled-out icing to this measurement to form a wall that slants downwards from the castle to the turret in an interesting fashion.

Add to the effect by curving the wall a little. The curve will also help to provide a snug fit; you can cut away small sections at either end of the wall to adjust it further if necessary.

Construct a similar wall between turrets numbers 1 and 2.

2 Form a long, fat sausage from soft icing. Cut it into two pieces, one for the parapet of each wall. Use a scalpel to cut small sections out of each to create a castellated effect.

3 Moisten the base of the parapets, then attach them to the tops of the two walls.

4 Roll out some soft icing into long, flat strips and make further parapets, as described in Step 2. Moisten the strips with a little water and attach them to the turrets. Five strips have been used on the sample Castle Cake.

Additional Touches

Stairs

1 With more soft icing form a staircase that descends from the top of the rectangular cake to the board. Use suitable tools – for example, a small ruler, a knife, a plastic spatula or the number 1 pottery tool – to fashion the steps and other details, such as the landing.

2 Allow the stairs to dry thoroughly before adding the final touch of colour.

Grass

1 Press a variety of green-toned soft icings in a garlic crusher to form blades of grass.

2 Scrape clumps of grass off the garlic crusher with a spatula, moisten their bases with water and brush them onto the board beside the building or wherever required.

Rocks

1 Combine 250 g of sugar with 60 ml of water in a small saucepan. Place the mixture over a medium heat and stir it occasionally until it becomes a thick syrup. Using a confectioner's thermometer to test the temperature of the syrup, bring the mixture to the hard ball stage (120°C).

2 Remove the syrup from the heat and stir in half a cup of royal icing and some food colouring, if the rocks are to be coloured. Alternatively, add half a cup of sifted icing sugar and one stiffly whipped egg white instead of the royal icing. If the latter method is used, have the ingredients ready before commencing. Stir the mixture very thoroughly, then pour it into a well-greased tin. When it has cooled, break it into different-sized pieces representing rocks.

3 Place the rocks around the castle, using the colour plate as a guide.

Sand

1 Divide 500 g of sugar into three. Place one portion in a food processor fitted with a mincing blade and add some black powdered food colouring. Use the pulse button until the sugar is evenly coloured and finer in texture. Repeat the procedure with the other two portions, adding yellow and ochre.

2 Mix the three coloured sugars together to create realistic-looking sand.

Colouring the Castle

All colouring of details on the castle is done with dry powdered food colouring and a dry brush.

1 Mix together black, brown and dark blue powdered food colourings or dusts.

2 Use a small, flat paintbrush to outline a hazy brick pattern on the lower sections of the castle with the combined colourings.

3 Brush the colour over the roof sections so that a mottled slate effect is achieved.

4 Using a large, soft-bristled brush, gently brush some of the colour over the building to create a weathered appearance. Allow powder to fall behind the parapets and onto the top of the first storey of the castle. Let a little powder fall on the steps, rocks, sand and grass to create a general illusion of age and to blend all the components of the scene together.

5 Use black colouring to darken the window spaces.

See colour plate

on page 35

Rainbow Cake

Many people dream of finding their 'pot of gold at the end of the rainbow'. Since this is a wish for prosperity and good times, a rainbow cake can be used to celebrate a retirement, a lottery win or an achievement that will ensure success and happiness.

The Rainbow Cake is a very easy cake to decorate. It can be made in any shape, although for obvious reasons a round cake is best. Use any of the cake recipes given in the Recipes chapter. Coverings of bought almond and soft icings have been used for the cake illustrated; however, a butter icing (see Recipes chapter) may be applied if the cake used is not a fruit one. The cake may be made in any size.

The cake illustrated required one quantity of cake mixture (250 g butter) and 1 kg of bought soft icing.

Covering the Cake

The cake is best covered in white icing to display the rainbow colours to greatest advantage.

Using Almond and Soft Icings

When the cake is cool, remove it from its tin and place it on a suitable presentation board. Follow the instructions given in the chapter on Covering the Cake for applying a bought almond, then a soft, icing. Allow the final covering to dry for a few days before completing the other decorations.

Using Butter Icing

1 Glaze the cake with a little warmed apricot jam or honey. Place the cake on a turntable; you can make a turntable from a circular board and a mug, if you do not own a manufactured one. Load a broad spatula with some butter icing, hold it upright and parallel to the side of the cake, then allow the cake to turn. The icing will spread evenly around the side of the cake as the turntable revolves. Repeat the process until the side of the cake has been completely covered. Smooth the edge of the top if any excess icing has gathered there.

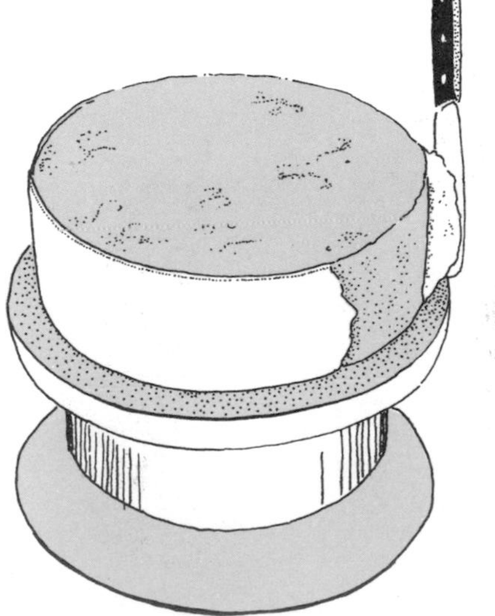

2 Using a spatula, place a line of icing across the diameter of the cake's top. Place the spatula parallel to the cake surface, with its tip at the centre. Allow the cake to turn. In this way the spatula will sweep the icing around the top of the cake. Repeat the process until the whole top is covered and smooth. Wipe away any excess icing.

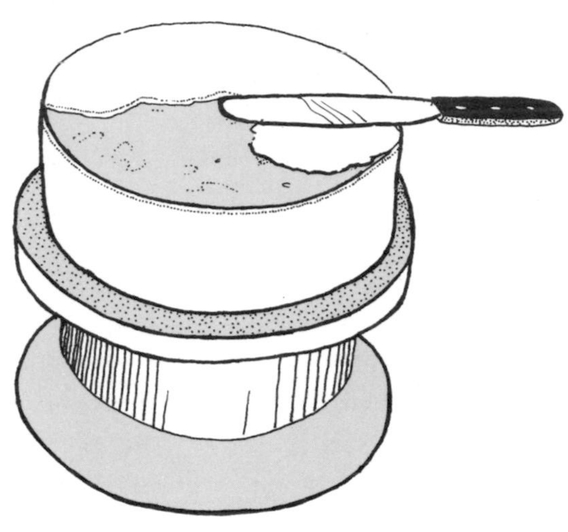

3 Place the cake on a suitable presentation board, using broad cake slides.

Making the Rainbow

1 The rainbow is made with piping jelly. Piping jelly is best purchased; however, a recipe is included in the Recipes chapter, in case you find it difficult to buy piping jelly. For economy, purchase a neutral rather than a coloured jelly.

Place a spoonful of piping jelly into seven sections of a patty tin. Add a drop of liquid food colouring to each and stir well. The colours of the rainbow are red, orange, yellow, green, blue, indigo and violet.

Rainbow Cake

(see page 33)

Face Masks

(see page 39)

2 On a piece of tracing paper, draw seven expanding arcs. A protractor is useful for this. Make the arcs a suitable size for your cake. Turn the paper over and trace along the lines of the arcs.

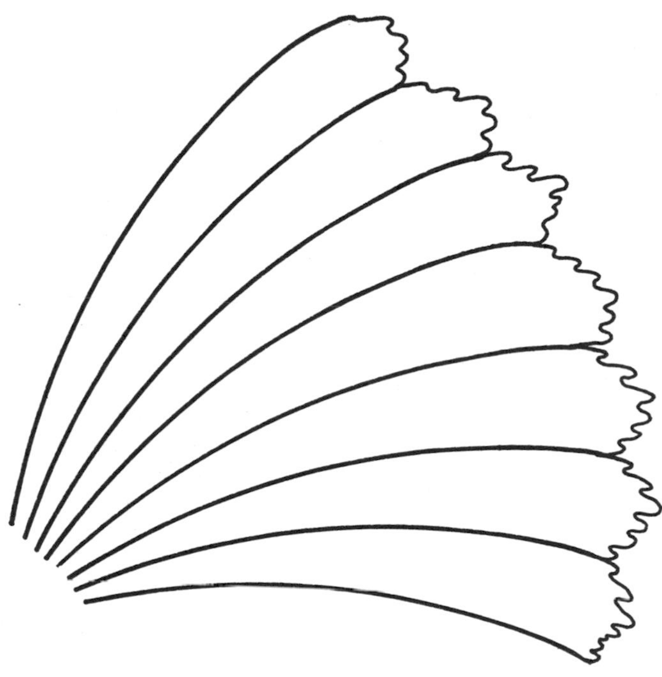

3 If the cake has been covered in soft icing, place the tracing paper on the cake and draw over the lines again. The lines traced on the back previously will be transferred to the cake's surface.

If a butter icing has been used, it will not be possible to work in this way, because the icing does not harden. In this case, either of the following two methods can be used.

Cut out all the sections between the drawn arcs. Place the first section on the surface of the cake and trace around it, using a skewer. Remove the piece and repeat the procedure for each of the sections.

Alternatively, the arcs can be drawn on one side of a piece of rice paper and the rainbow cut out along its outline. Brush the back of the cut-out rainbow with just a little egg white, but be careful because too much moisture can destroy rice paper. Place the rainbow on the cake and press it down gently. Fill the sections between the arcs with coloured piping jelly as described in Step 4.

4 Both a large and a small sable paintbrush are needed to brush jelly into the larger and smaller parts of the sections. Commence with red in the outside, top section and continue through the range of colours. Allow the colours to merge a little where they change, because this will give the rainbow a more realistic appearance. If preferred, it is possible to pipe the jelly into the sections, then use a brush to spread it. Note that piping jelly never sets very hard so, although it has a skin, it will still show finger marks if it is touched.

Decorating the Side

1 Brush a series of small piping jelly rainbows around the side of the cake. These are so small that they are best done freehand.

2 The rainbows hold in place better if they start and finish in small clouds. The clouds prevent the jelly from running down the side of the cake while it is setting.

Make a quantity of firm-peak royal icing (see Recipes chapter). Use a paper-cone bag and a number 8 star tube (see Equipment chapter) to pipe a small amount of icing at both ends of each rainbow. Use a paintbrush moistened with water to brush down the icing to create a cloud effect.

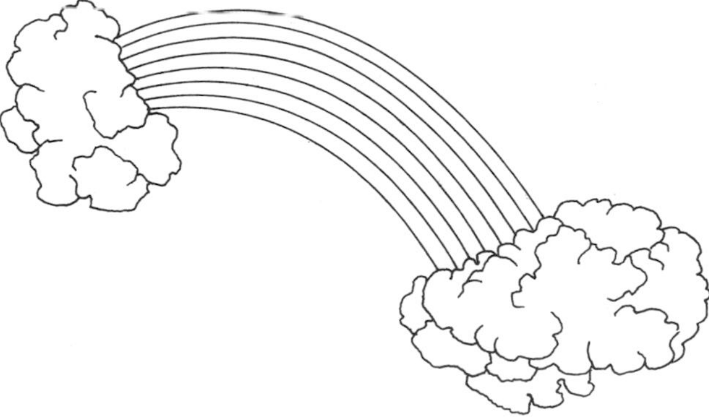

3 Set the cake aside to allow the decorations to dry a little.

Pot of Gold

Make the pot of gold a suitable size for your cake. Use gum paste (see Recipes chapter) to make the pot and the coins.

1 Work up a quantity of gum paste until it is firm but still pliable. Roll out a small ball of the paste to form a 2-mm-thick circle about 8 cm in diameter. Trim the edge if it has become ragged.

2 Place a small wad of cotton wool in the centre of the circle to help the pot keep its shape, then draw up the circle around it. Mould the pot to a good, rounded shape. Pinch and squeeze it into shape at the top.

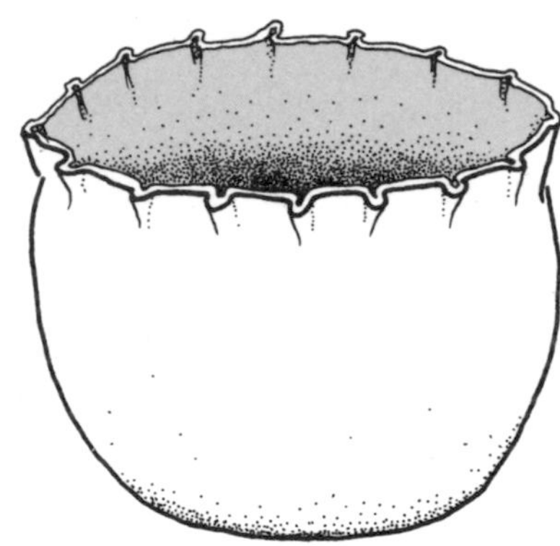

3 Place the pot on a bed of cornflour for a few days to allow it to dry. When the pot is dry, use a pair of tweezers to remove the wad of cotton wool.

4 Roll out some more paste to a thickness of 2 mm. Use a small circular cutter to cut out a large number of coins. Place the coins on a bed of cornflour for a few days to dry.

5 Use a paintbrush moistened with methylated spirits to paint the coins and the pot with gold dusting powder. Note that the coins need to be coloured on both sides. It is also sometimes necessary to give them a second coat of colouring, because gold paint tends to brush off as it dries.

6 Brush a little royal icing on the base of the pot to ensure that it will stay in place, then add the pot to the cake as shown in the colour plate. Insert a wad of gold-coloured cotton wool in the pot and sprinkle coins on top. Allow some coins to spill over part of the cake and the presentation board.

Shell Edge

A running shell edge can be piped at the base, between the cake and the board, to complete the design. Use the colour plate as a guide to the appearance of the finished edge.

1 Fit a paper-cone bag with a number 8 star tube. Fill the bag with firm-peak royal icing.

2 Hold the bag so that the tip of the tube is at the base of the cake and the bag forms a 45-degree angle to both the cake and the board. Press the bag to release the icing. Allow the icing to run in a straight line for about 1 cm; still pressing on the bag, let the icing build up a little, then move along another 1 cm. Repeat the procedure until you have an unbroken edge all around the base of the cake. If, for some reason, a join is required the edges of the join can be brushed down with a moistened brush.

If a finer edge is required, use a number 5 star tube.

See colour plate

on page 36

Face Masks

All the world's a stage, and all the men and women merely players:
They have their exits and their entrances;
And one man in his time plays many parts

William Shakespeare, *As You Like It*

Whether young or old, conservative or outrageous, we all sometimes feel like kicking up our heels. When we are in such a mood, we want our celebrations to involve something more than just the usual round or square, birthday-style cake. The Face Masks shown in the colour plate are suitably different cakes for these occasions. The Face Masks are also ideal because they can symbolise the many faces we don – the faces we hide behind and the faces we assume to act out the different parts life forces us to play.

Adapt the cakes to suit the person and the celebration. The cakes can portray dramatic theatre masks, happy or sad clowns or just amusing characters. The only limitations to these cakes are those of the creator.

The contours of the faces are built up first, before they are covered with bought soft icing. Because of the heaviness of the built-up icing, it is best to use a fruit cake recipe. The cakes do not require a covering of almond icing before the soft icing layer, because the faces have already been substantially contoured with almond icing.

The two masks illustrated require one quantity of cake mixture (250 g butter) and 2 kg of bought soft icing.

Shaping the Cakes

The easiest way to make the mask cakes is to use small or medium, oval-shaped tins. Small cakes are best, because their proportions look the most lifelike. The cakes shown in the colour plate have been baked in small, 15-cm tins.

1 Make up one quantity of cake mixture (see Recipes chapter) and divide it between two small, oval tins. Bake the cakes according to the instructions.

2 Remove the cakes from the tins once they have cooled. Use some royal icing (see Recipes chapter) scraped on their bases to anchor them to a suitable presentation board. Use some bought almond icing to fill in any holes around the sides of the cakes, but do not worry about the top.

3 Use photographs to help you model the masks. If no pictures are available, you will have to use your own face! Carefully examine your facial structure and contours in a hand mirror before beginning work.

The face cakes should be seen as dividing into thirds. The top section is the forehead and eyes, the middle contains the nose and cheeks and the bottom section includes the mouth and chin.

4 Knead and warm some bought almond icing with your hands. It is very important to do this so that the icing is at its most pliable.

Use pottery tools when you come to make lines and markings (see Equipment chapter). Small spatulas are useful for smoothing and pressing the icing into position and ensuring it remains firmly in place.

Build up a suitable ridge for the forehead on one cake. The highest part forms the eyebrows. The forehead curves and softens towards the hairline. Do not forget to include the creases and folds formed when a person laughs, frowns or is caught by surprise.

5 Decide what shape the nose is to be and build up the ridge accordingly. The build up should meet at the forehead. Smooth the joins, then ease the icing down either side of the nose. Press indentations into the icing for the nostrils.

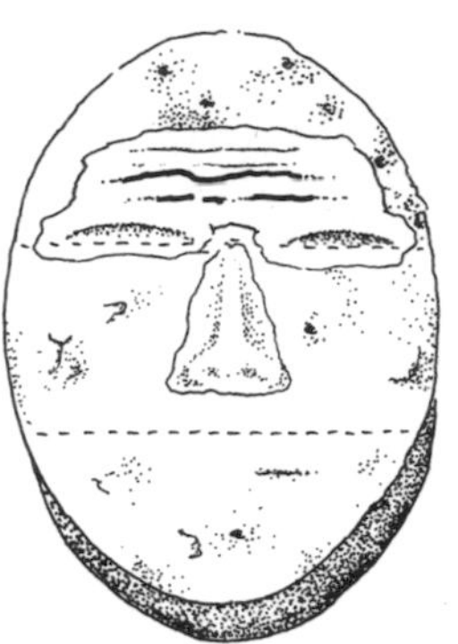

6 Build up the cheekbones, taking into account whether the face is to be sad or happy. If, for example, the face is to be happy, the build up is at its fullest to the sides of the face, below the eyes. Use pottery tools and a spatula to smooth and shape the areas. Form dimples if you want them. Build up some icing slightly to form the areas around the mouth. Shape the section below the nose as well as the area immediately below the lower lip.

7 Use more icing to build up the chin, easing the icing down to the edge of the oval.

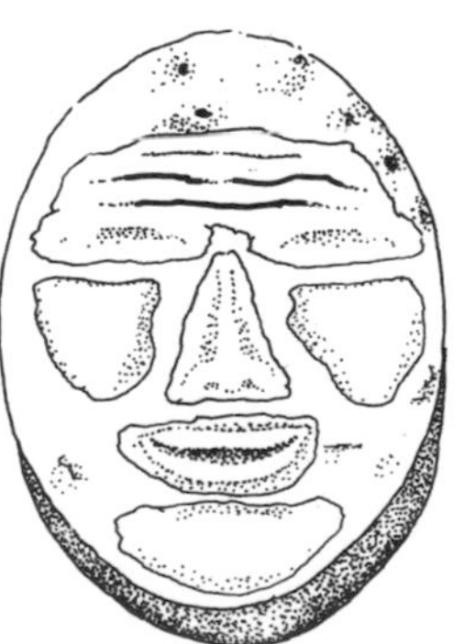

8 The eyes are best left as depressions, but you will need to spread a little icing in the depressions to keep the transition between the contours of the forehead area smooth. Slant the eye sockets so that they express emotion, such as happiness.

9 Repeat Steps 4–8 for the second mask cake.

10 Set the cakes aside for at least a week to dry thoroughly.

Covering the Cakes

Colour enough soft icing to cover both the cakes. Tan tones make the best base for the detailed colouring added when the icing of the cakes is completed.

Glaze the cakes with egg white, then apply the icing in the way described in the chapter on Covering the Cake. The face contours remain even when the covering is placed over them. Do not make the covering icing too thick, otherwise the face proportions will be too exaggerated.

Headpieces

Left-hand Face Mask

The cake on the left in the colour plate has been decorated with three bands of fluted icing.

1 Colour three small amounts of soft icing brown, orange and red.

2 Make the brown icing into a long, fat sausage, then roll this out to a strip long enough to encircle the top of the head. Cut the strip to a width of 2.5–3 cm. Use the cornfloured handle of a paintbrush to flute one long edge of the strip: roll it along the edge until the icing stretches and curls, creating a frill. Moisten a line across the brow with water and position the strip along this. The strip becomes the back frill of the headpiece. Press the icing where it joins the brow, then place some cotton wool balls behind the frill so that it stands out from the head. Allow the band to dry for a few hours before you make the second strip.

3 Use the orange icing to form the second frill. This is made in the same way as the first, but make the strip 3–3.5 cm wide. Flute then apply the second layer along a moistened line on the brow, in front of the first frill. Once again place some small cotton wool balls behind the icing to help it stand out from the cake. Allow a few hours' drying time before making the final frill.

4 Make the red strip 2.5–3 cm wide and repeat the procedure described for the brown and orange frills. Allow at least 1 cm of the orange frill to show above the red layer.

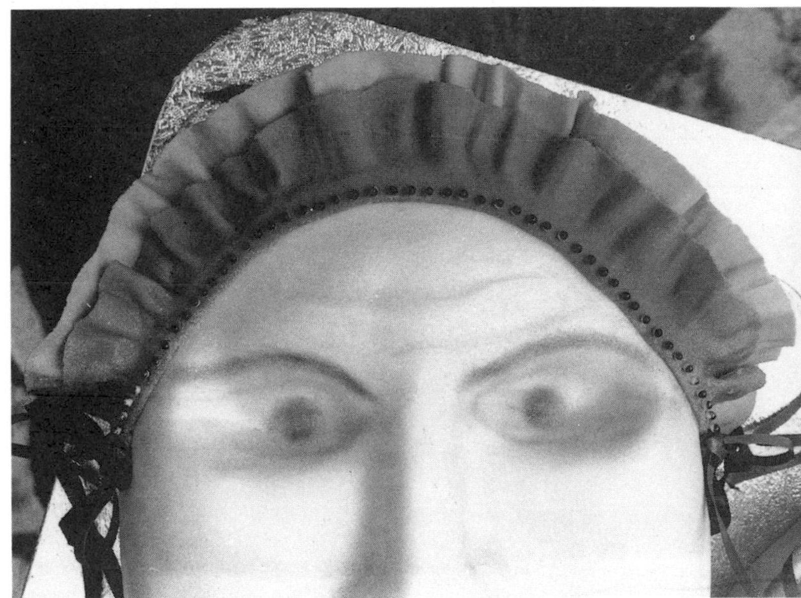

5 Use some suitably coloured stamens to decorate the lower part of the red frill. The cake on the left was decorated with large, two-toned (maroon and yellow), shiny stamens. Because the stamens are so large and shiny, they look like beading when placed in a row. Cut the stamens into short lengths and insert them into the icing while it is still soft. Ensure the spacing between them is uniform.

6 Use 1 m of thin, brown fabric ribbon and one of red to complete the headpiece. Cut the ribbons in half. Knot a brown length and a red together at their centres and repeat the procedure for the second pair of ribbons to produce two adornments with four tails each. Use a pair of scissors to curl the ends of the ribbons by running a blade along them. Then use some royal icing to attach the adornments to either side of the frills, so that they look like mask ribbons.

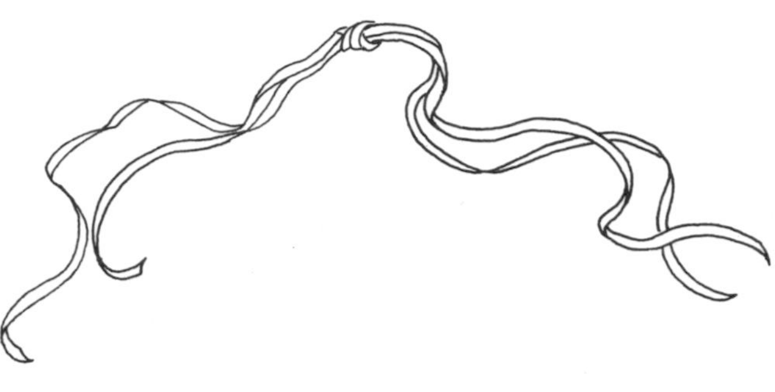

Right-hand Face Mask

The second mask has been decorated with strips of curled icing that are held in place with a headband.

1 Colour six small amounts of soft icing red, orange, pink, green, brown and tan. Shape the orange icing into four long, thin sausages. Roll them out into strips about 1 cm in width. Moisten the underside of one strip at one end, then place it on the forehead. Press it firmly to ensure it adheres to the cake. Twist and turn the strip so that it falls in a long curl. Arrange the rest of the orange strips as desired.

2 Roll out each of the other coloured icings in the same way. Arrange these strips in curls, also, so that when they have all been placed the head appears to have multi-coloured hair.

3 Roll out a long, 2–3-cm-wide piece of red soft icing. Cut a headband from this (perhaps copying the style shown in the colour plate), then moisten the bottom edge with a little water. Place the headband on the forehead so that it appears to hold the hair in place. Insert a number of gold cashews along the band.

4 Take 1 m of narrow, green ribbon and another metre of gold ribbon. Cut them in half. Make two pairs of green and gold ribbons, then tie them at their centres so that both have four tails. Curl the ends as you did the ends of the ribbons for the left-hand mask. Use royal icing to attach both pairs just below the hairband, on either side of the face.

Colouring the Completed Faces

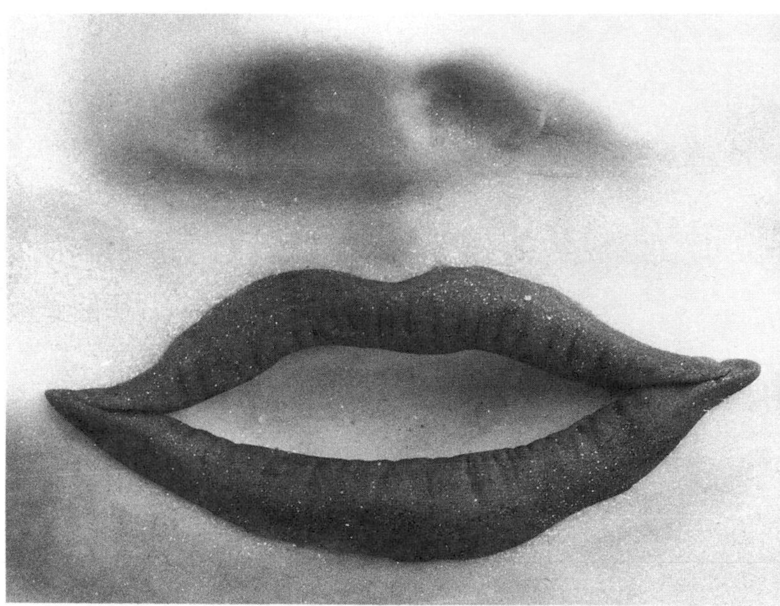

The two masks may be coloured in the same tones or differently, as in the case of the faces in the colour plate. Use petal dust for the colouring, including at least one petal dust that has a glitter or frosted effect, so that the faces take on a festive appearance.

1 Brush the cheeks with colour, ensuring different parts receive dark and soft tones to create the illusion of the play of light and shade. This work is very much like putting on make-up, so use the same wide brush strokes and a large, soft-bristled paintbrush. Brush some colour around the nostril area and below the nose. A little extra colour may be brushed onto parts of the chin and also below the eyes, if desired.

2 Use a combination of black, deep blue and a glitter blue to brush in the eyebrows, eyes and other eye details. The eyelid areas may be large enough to allow colour to be added like eyeshadow: if so, apply the colour with brush strokes that draw it right to the outer edges of the eye areas.

3 Take a small amount of soft icing and colour it suitably for lips. Apply two small, shaped bands to the faces to represent the lips of a mouth. Lips should be pressed into an expression that matches that of the rest of the face. Make some small crease lines in the covering icing on either side of the pairs of lips so that the mouths look realistic.

See colour plate

on page 54

Baobab Tree Cake

The baobab, boab or bottle tree is a most unusual and little-known tree. It grows in north-western Australia and parts of the Northern Territory; it is also found in South Africa. The tree produces a mantle of leaves only once every two years so it is more commonly recognised in its bare state. The very portly shape of the trunk gives it its name of bottle tree. Its shape and its immense size make it an ideal subject for a child's fantasy bushland cake. The Baobab Tree Cake would also be ideal for welcoming or farewelling an overseas traveller.

The Baobab Tree Cake shown in the colour plate houses many Australian bush creatures that do not usually appear together but add interest and fantasy to the cake. A pair of kookaburras and a pair of galahs, in addition to a number of rosellas, perch in the branches. A possum and her baby can be seen, as well as a koala – a most unlikely occupant. The base of the tree has been decorated with anthills, rocks, a pair of frill-necked lizards and a jabiru (native stork). The tree is placed on a bed of two-toned sugar sand.

Use a fruit cake recipe (see Recipes chapter) because the cake needs to be firm enough to support all the branches and animals. The cake illustrated required one quantity of cake mixture (250 g butter) and 2–2.5 kg of bought soft icing.

Shaping the Cake

1 The shape can be achieved in two ways: either bake the mixture in a new, clean, terracotta plant pot; or use a suitably shaped container made from foil.

If you choose the first way, select a small terracotta pot with a diameter of 12–16 cm. Terracotta pots are ovenproof, so cakes can be baked in them quite safely. Grease the inside of the pot, then sprinkle a coating of plain flour over the greased base and sides. Bake the fruit cake as instructed in the Recipes chapter.

If you choose to fashion a container, use a

large, heavy-duty foil tray. Smooth out its rolled edges so that it is almost flat. Place an ovenproof saucer or some other suitable item at its centre to form the base of the shape. With a pair of scissors make a series of cuts in the foil from its edges to the saucer's rim, to create a windmill-like effect. Partly overlap the strips and staple them together as you work around the shape. The foil strips should overlap more at the top of the mould than at the base, so that the mould takes on a rounded shape. Place a tray beneath the mould when you bake the cake and also tie some string around its middle so that it does not burst open during cooking.

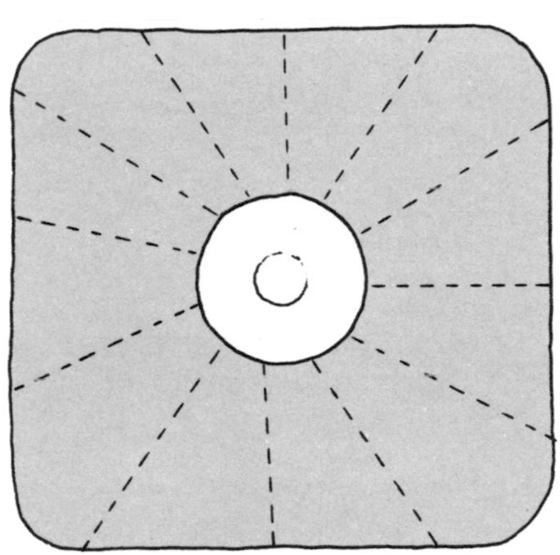

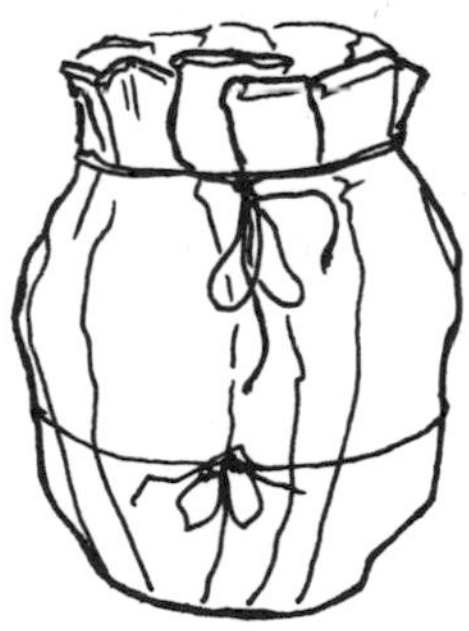

2 When the baked cake has cooled, remove it from the plant pot or foil mould.

3 If a pot was used, cut away some of the cake so that the diameter of the base is narrower than that of the middle. It is not necessary to patch and fill the holes of the Baobab Tree Cake because its surface does not have to be smooth. It is, however, necessary to build up sections of the cake so that it takes on a bottle shape (see Step 4).

4 Knead some bought almond icing in your hands until it is soft and pliable. If your cake does not have a bulge press a band of icing around its middle to achieve this. Build up ridges to give the trunk character.

Covering the Cake

1 Glaze the cake with warmed apricot jam. Roll out some almond icing to a rectangle long enough to fit around the tree and wide enough to cover the cake to its top. Place the cake on the icing, then roll it along the length. Press the icing at the join and cut away any excess at the top and base of the cake.

2 Scrape some royal icing (see Recipes chapter) onto a presentation board and place the cake in position.

Branches

1 To make the branches, use a number of pieces of heavy cotton-covered wire. The Baobab Tree Cake in the colour plate has been given seven branches. Twist several wires together to form a support for the icing and creatures of each branch. Make each combination of twisted wires a different length and ensure that the ones for longer branches are thicker to provide better support.

Cover each support with stretched florists' tape, so that when it is inserted in the trunk it will not contaminate the cake.

2 Insert the covered-wire supports in the top of the cake. It may be necessary to push as much as one-third of each support into the cake to ensure each branch is stable and unable to fall out. Bend and curve the supports to make them look realistic and to create positions for the animals and birds that will sit in the branches.

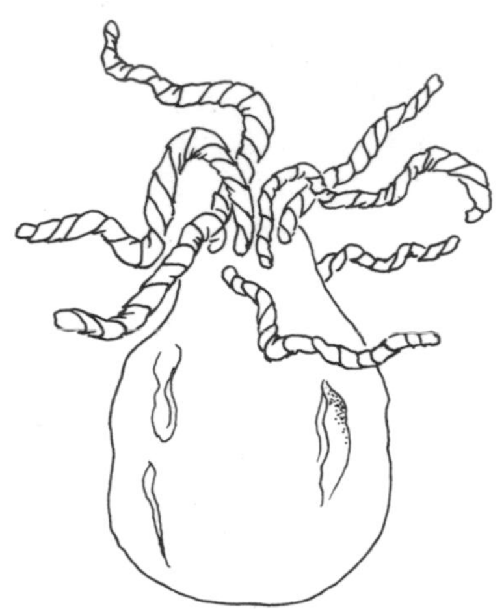

3 Colour some soft icing in a suitable shade of brownish grey. Roll out the icing to a rectangle long enough to go around the tree and wide enough to cover the cake to the top. Glaze the cake with egg white. Roll the icing into a cylinder. Place the roll upright against the side of the cake, then work around the cake, unrolling the icing as you do so. Press the icing so that it adheres to the side of the cake. Cut away any excess at the join. Press and squeeze some of the excess icing at the top of the cake along the start of the branches to increase their stability and to create natural-looking bulges. Make indentations in the icing suggesting ridges and marks to give the tree character.

4 Gather up any leftover soft icing and knead it well until it becomes soft and pliable. Moisten the wire branch supports, then press and squeeze some icing onto them. The wires need to be completely covered with icing. The branches should be thick where they join the trunk and thin at their extremities.

5 Allow the completed tree to dry thoroughly for a week or two before colouring.

Colouring the Tree

Use a combination of black, brown, frosted orange and rust for the tree's final colouring. Place a small amount of each colour, plus 1 teaspoon of cornflour, on a small plate. Combine a little of each colour, adding just a fraction of the cornflour. Brush the composite colour over the cake with a soft-bristled paintbrush (see Equipment chapter). Use the remaining, unmixed portions for odd splashes of colour here and there. Patches of rust and black will help you achieve a natural effect.

Birds, Animals and Objects

Anthills

1 Colour some soft icing dull orange. Knead it into three tall, pointed, cone-like pieces, each of a different height.

2 Scrape a little royal icing on the bases of the anthills and set them in position on the presentation board.

3 Use a pottery tool (see Equipment chapter) to make creases and folds in each, so that they look like anthills. Use photographs of anthills and the colour plate to assist you with these markings.

Rocks

Refer to the chapter on the Castle Cake for instructions on how to make rocks.

Grass

The small patches of grass placed beside the rocks are made in the way described for the leaves in the Grass Trees chapter.

Frill-necked Lizards

1 Knead some orange-coloured soft icing until it is soft and pliable. Shape it into two long, pointed cones 4 cm in length and about 3 cm in diameter at their widest part.

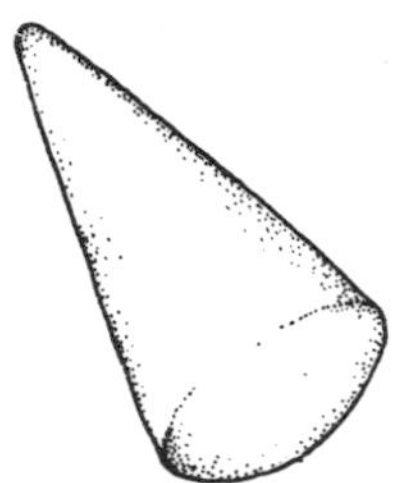

2 Form small, pointed heads at the wide ends of the cones. Pinch out a frill for each on either side of its face. The frills do not extend below the faces and they have a division at the top centre. Pull and press the pointed ends of the two cones to form long, tapering bodies and tails.

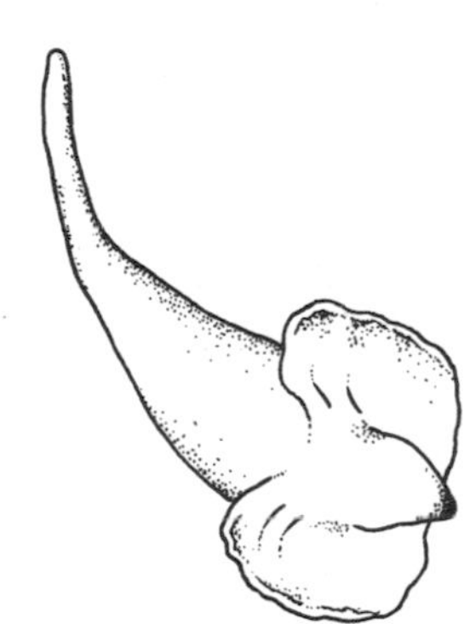

3 Take a little more icing and form four pairs of legs, two for each lizard. Use a pair of scissors to cut small, claw-like divisions for the feet. Moisten the legs where they will join the bodies, then press them into position on the lizards.

4 Position the lizards close together on the rocks. Use your pottery tools to make features, such as eyes and mouths, in the faces.

Jabiru

1 Take some black-coloured soft icing and a little white soft icing. Knead the black icing into a fat football shape then pull and squeeze out one end of this to form the bird's neck and head, making sure you allow for a pointed beak.

2 The jabiru's markings are created by flattening small sections of white icing with your fingers and applying them to the bird's body. Moisten the bird's breast area, then press a small rectangle of white icing onto it. Press and smooth the icing until it takes on the appearance of white breast markings. Repeat the procedure for the top of the back and the outsides of the wings. When the bird is complete, use your pottery tools to mark on features, such as the eyes.

3 Position the bird on the board, using a little royal icing.

Kookaburras

1 Mould a small quantity of brown soft icing into two small, rather pointed football shapes. Use your fingers to mould an end of each into a head and beak. Pull out the other ends of both shapes a little, then press and squeeze them to form the tails.

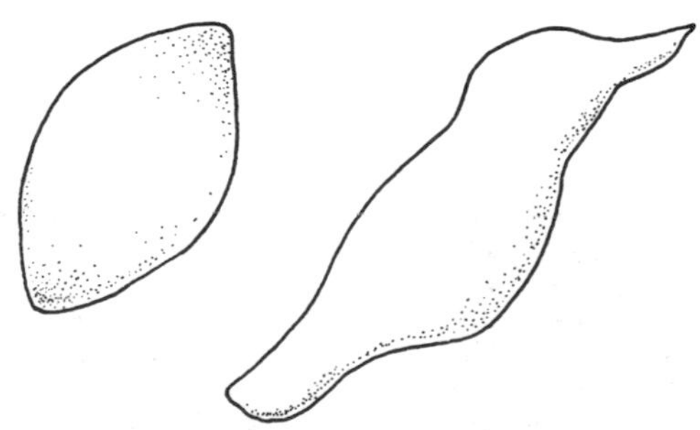

2 Use the methods described in Step 2 for the jabiru to create the birds' markings. Place small pieces of bluish white icing on the tops and sides of the heads, on the breasts and on the outsides of the wings. Press the pieces to ensure they merge with the bodies of the birds. Use pottery tools to make markings for the beaks, wings and eyes.

3 Position the birds on the tree with a little royal icing.

Galahs

1 The heads, fronts and bases of the two birds are made of pink soft icing; the remainder of the bodies is grey. Press the two coloured icings together to make the birds. If the juxtaposition of colours does not look quite right, use a small pair of scissors to cut out the inappropriate bits of icing.

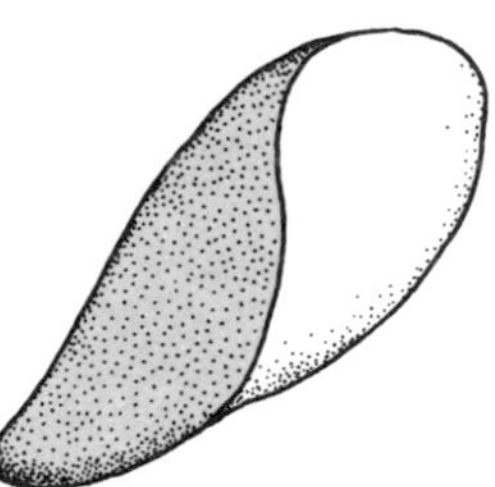

2 Use pottery tools to make eyes and wings in the icing. Press some of the icing at the tops of the two shapes to form the birds' heads. Use a pair of scissors to cut a very small crest for each.

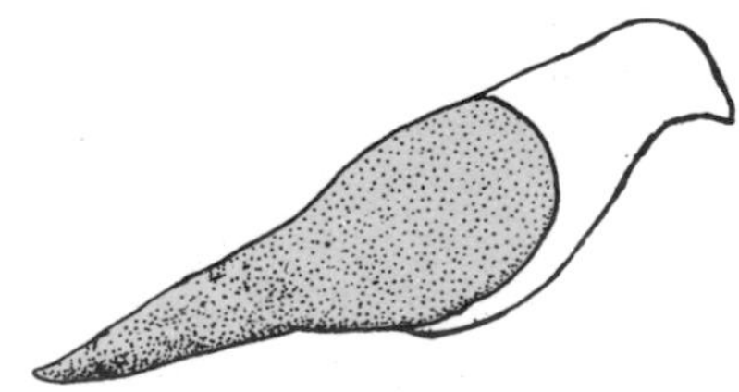

3 Position the birds on the tree, using a little royal icing to secure them.

Rosellas

1 Take small amounts of red and green soft icing. Make nine small footballs from the green icing. Press a small, narrow strip of red icing on either side of each body to represent wings. Shape the nine pieces of icing with your hands into birds. Pull the icing at one end of each to make a tail, and pinch a little at the other to form a head and beak.

2 Use pottery tools to make eyes in the heads.

3 Place the rosellas on several branches of the baobab, using a little royal icing to secure them.

Possums

1 Form two football shapes from a small amount of pale brown soft icing; one should be larger than the other.

2 Cut into the shapes with a pair of scissors to form legs.

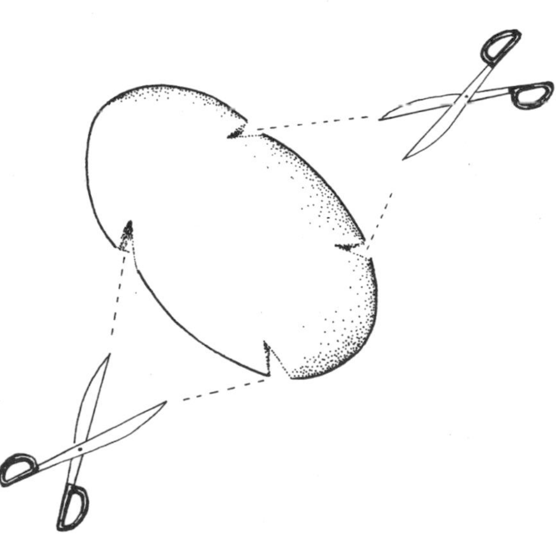

3 Pinch out a tail at one end of each shape and use your hands and fingers to form a head at the other.

4 Pinch out a pair of small ears and a little pointed mouth for each possum. Use pottery tools to make eyes and snouts in the faces.

5 Pull out the tail of each to form a long, thin curl. Mould the legs to a suitable shape and use a pair of scissors to make small claws for the feet. Position the possums so that the small baby rides on the mother's back. Use a little royal icing to secure the two in the tree. Allow their tails to rest curled on one of the branches so that they will not break off.

Koala

1 Form some grey soft icing into a small, squat cylinder. Use your fingers to form the koala's head. Cut the four limbs from the main body of icing, using a small pair of scissors.

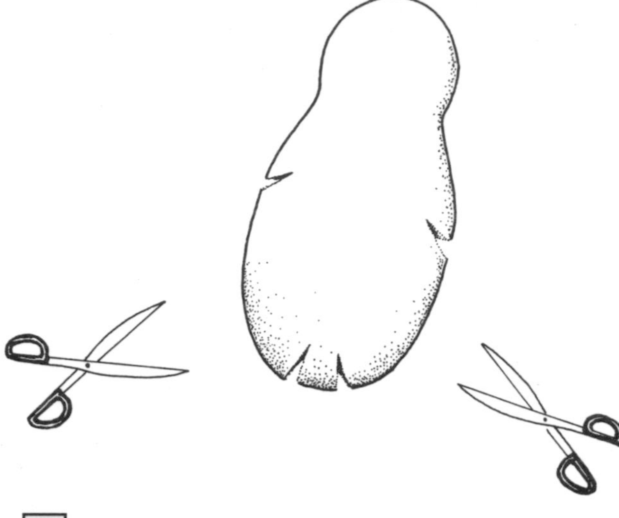

2 Pinch out a pair of ears at the top of the head. Use pottery tools to make eyes in the face. Place a small knob of black icing on the face for the nose.

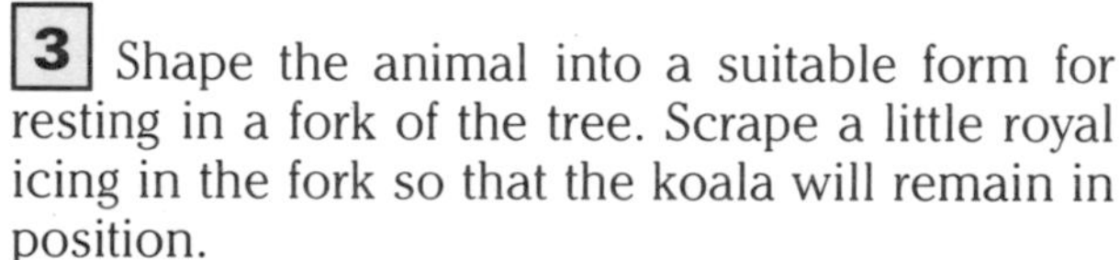

3 Shape the animal into a suitable form for resting in a fork of the tree. Scrape a little royal icing in the fork so that the koala will remain in position.

Lizard

1 Shape a small amount of brownish orange soft icing into a thin sausage about 5 cm in length.

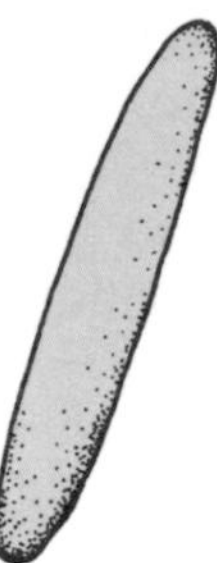

2 Pull one end a little to form a pointed tail, then shape the other end to form a slightly pointed head.

3 Scrape a little royal icing on the base of the lizard and position it on the tree so that it looks as if it is resting partly in a hollow to one side.

Sugar Sand

Once everything has been placed in position, the final touch – sand in the area surrounding the tree – is added. This will give a more natural appearance to the scene. See the chapter on the Castle Cake for instructions about how to make the coloured sand. Make the sand in gold as well as orange, then merge the two on the board.

See colour plate

on page 53

Swans

These cakes have a wonderfully delicate and fragile appearance. They are suitable for weddings, engagements or valentine celebrations. The Swans shown in the colour plate have been formed from two small, 15-cm, oval fruit cakes. It is best to use a fruit cake mixture because the decorating is slow and time-consuming, so other cakes would become stale.

Each of the swans illustrated required half a quantity of cake mixture (125 g butter) and 1.5 kg of bought soft icing.

Shaping the Cakes

1 Bake two small, oval fruit cakes (see Recipes chapter) and allow them to stand for a few days before commencing work. This will ensure they become sufficiently firm not to break and crumble when being shaped.

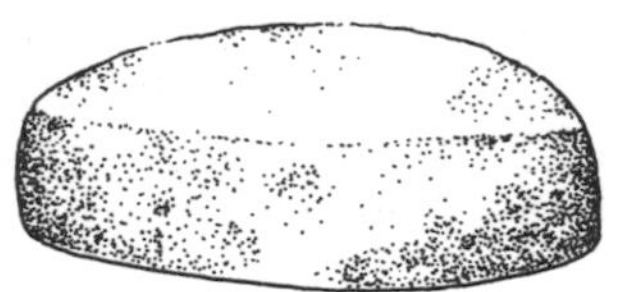

2 Cut away small sections of one cake with a sharp knife to form a curving slope at one of the ends. Repeat the procedure for the second cake, making sure the two are identical.

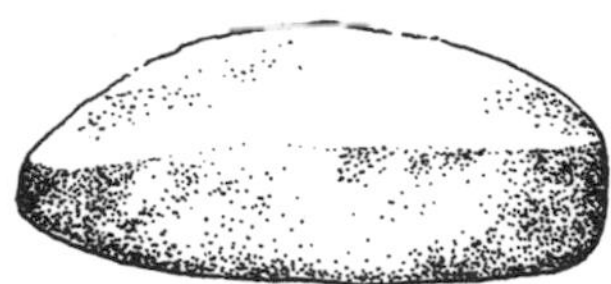

3 Use a little bought almond icing to fill and patch any holes and depressions in the sides and top of each cake.

4 Glaze both cakes with warmed apricot jam. Roll out some almond icing and cover each cake with a thin layer, following the instructions given in the chapter on Covering the Cake.

5 Allow the almond icing to dry for a week so that it becomes firm. In the meantime, make the supports for the swans' necks.

6 Take a piece of thick wire – the wire used for coat hangers is suitable – and bend and curve it into a figure 2. The base needs to be long enough for a minimum of 8 cm to be inserted into the cake. The top section represents the curve of the swan's upper neck, head and beak. The wire needs to be 19 cm high, 10–11 cm long at the base and 9 cm wide across the top curve. Make a second support in the same way.

7 Wrap several strands of heavy cotton-covered wire around both figure 2 wires to make them thicker. Cover the two supports with white florists' tape. Ensure that the ends that are to be inserted into the cakes are well covered and will not unravel, causing contamination of the cake.

8 Choose a suitable, foil-covered presentation board. Scrape a little royal icing (see Recipes chapter) on the bases of both cakes, then position them on the board.

9 Insert a wire neck support into the lower, shaped end of each cake. Use some soft icing to build up the base area of each swan where the wire has been inserted to help support the wire and to suggest the shape of the bird's breast.

Smooth the sides and rears of the birds with cake scrapers. The sections around the base of the swans' necks will also need to be smoothed and shaped appropriately. Not all the excess icing should be trimmed away: some can be effectively used to improve the shape.

Covering the Cakes

1 Glaze both cakes with egg white.

Roll out some white soft icing and cover one bird's body with it, following the instructions given in the chapter on Covering the Cake.

Colour some soft icing with black powdered food colouring. If the powder appears to be green based, add some brown. The powder should be kneaded into a small ball of the icing, which is then kneaded into the larger mass. Roll out the black icing and cover the second swan in the way you did the white bird.

2 Moisten the white swan's wire neck. Cover it with white soft icing to an appropriate thickness. Ensure the top of the neck tapers, then forms a head and beak, using the colour plate as a guide.

Repeat the procedure for the black swan, using black soft icing.

3 Insert three bamboo skewers into the top of each bird's rear. The skewers should be 1 cm apart.

Make a suitably sized, cone-shaped tail from white soft icing and moisten the wide end with a little water. Push the wide end onto the skewers so that the tail adheres to the cake surface. Knead and push the cone until it has formed a tail 5 cm long by 5 cm wide where it joins the body.

Swans

(*see page 51*)

Baobab Tree Cake

(see page 44)

Give the black swan a black icing tail in the same way.

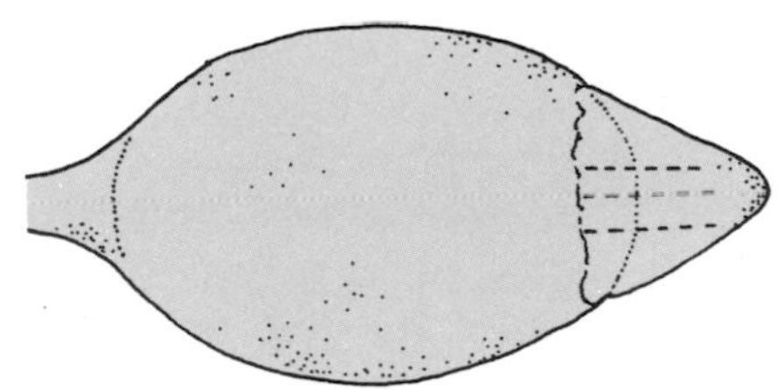

Adding the Swans' Plumage

The plumage, like the covering of the bodies, is made from coloured soft icing: white for the first swan, brownish black for the second. The feathers of the head, neck and breast are assembled first, then those of the tail area, and finally the long feathers of the back and wing parts.

1 Mould some white soft icing into two shallow crescents and place one on either side of the centre of the white swan's back. The two pieces will help you to recreate the two high, curving ridges of feathers that can be seen on the top of a swan's back. The crescents should be about 11 cm in length and 6 cm at their widest width (midway, where they curve).

Give the black swan two crescents in the same way.

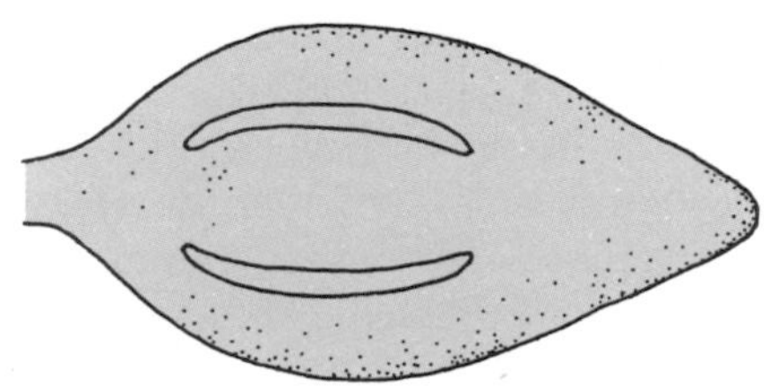

2 Use the following patterns to make the cutters numbered 1 to 11 for the swans' feathers (see the instructions on making cutters given in the Equipment chapter). Cutters 1–8 can be purchased, if you do not wish to make them, but cutters 9–11 must be made.

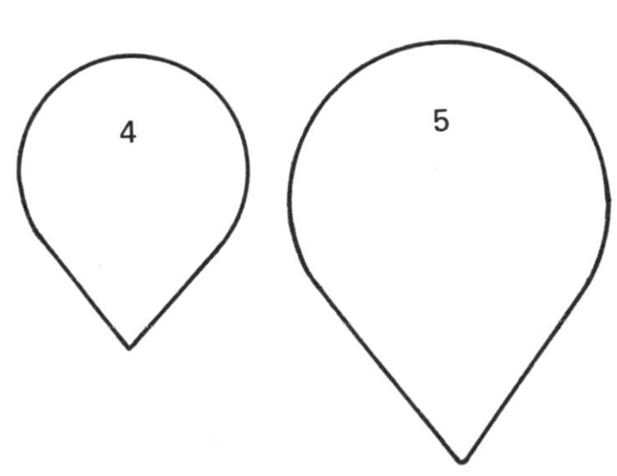

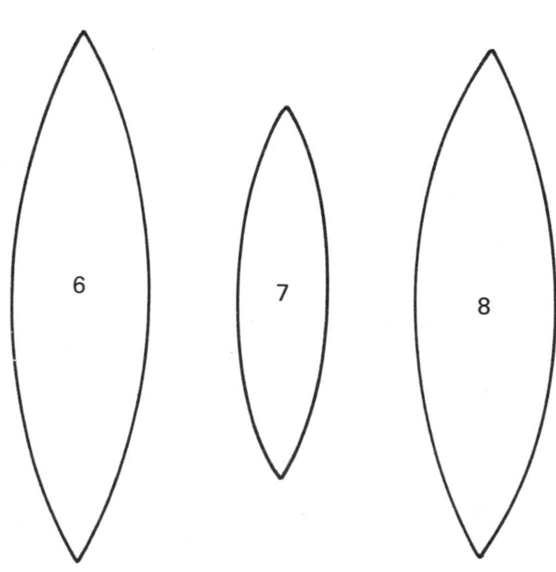

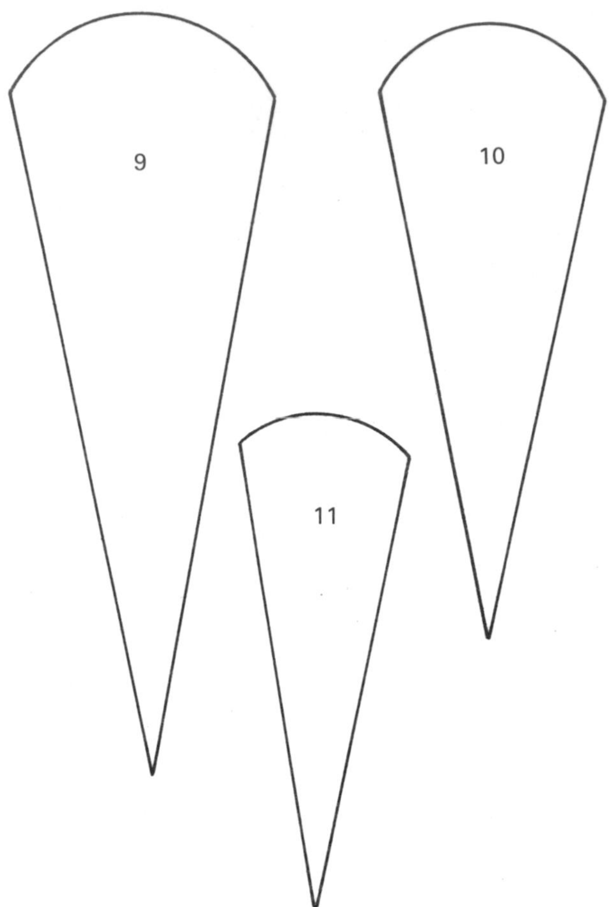

Start at the base of the breast and work towards the middle. The width of the areas on either side of the centre line is 5–6 cm. Overlap the feathers more and more as they progress towards the centre. The central feather is placed upright with the point placed downwards. Do not press down too firmly on the wide tops of the base feathers. Rather, allow them to sit out from the bird so that they look a little ruffled.

Once both sides of the base have been worked, start to place the rest of the feathers, working from the top to the base. Make a central vertical line of feathers, then place the rest of the feathers facing left on one side of the central row and right on the other. The second last row tucks under the rapidly drying base row, and so on, so that it is not possible to see the base of any feathers. If necessary, use a dry paintbrush gently to push the tops of each feather so that they stand out from the breast and neck.

5 Place a few more feathers on either side of the worked area of the breast to extend the width by 2 cm on each side. The feathers are made in the same way as the last lot; however, this time, press and squeeze each one so that it enlarges. Moisten and position the feathers in the same way you did the earlier ones. Ensure the base, pointed part of each is tucked under the previous one.

6 Assemble the ruff of feathers that is seen behind the neck on the body beyond the breast area already covered with feathers. Use the number 3 cutter to cut out the feathers. Elongate them by pressing and squeezing the icing. Or you may find it easier to use the handle of a paintbrush to elongate them. Roll the handle along the length of each feather.

These feathers go, in less symmetrical rows than the previous ones, between the small feathers already in place and the large feathers further back that are added later. So some of the ruff feathers may need to be added later, after the

3 Work a little cornflour into a piece of the white icing about the size of a golf ball, so that it does not become too soft and sticky during handling. Roll it out as thinly as possible. Using the number 1 cutter, cut out a number of feathers for the white swan's neck. Moisten the back of each with a little water, then apply them to the neck. Start at the back of the head and work all the way down the neck, making sure you also place feathers under the head. Use the colour plate as a guide.

The feathers should overlap each other. As you work down the length of the neck, overlap the feathers less so that they appear to be getting larger as they descend.

4 The last 5–6 cm of the neck, where icing has been built up previously, is covered with larger feathers: use the number 2 cutter. Moisten the back of the feathers with water.

large feathers have been positioned. Overlap the feathers and allow their tops to stand out from the body to create the ruffled effect.

7 To make some of the smaller feathers of the tail area use the number 4 cutter and cut out six petal-shaped feathers. Place one on a hard part of your hand and use the handle of a paintbrush to flute it: move the handle back and forth until the icing has thinned, then repeat the movement around the curved edge of the feather – as the icing becomes thinner this will curl and frill. Frill the other feathers. Moisten the backs of all and place them so that there are four on the sides of the tail (two on one side and two on the other) and one is on either side of the top of the tail. Be sure to cover the pointed bases of the feathers with subsequently added feathers.

8 Cut out one of the larger feathers of the tail area, using the number 5 cutter. Frill and flute it, then moisten its base. Place it on the top of the tail, in the centre. The fluted top of the feather faces to the rear of the bird.

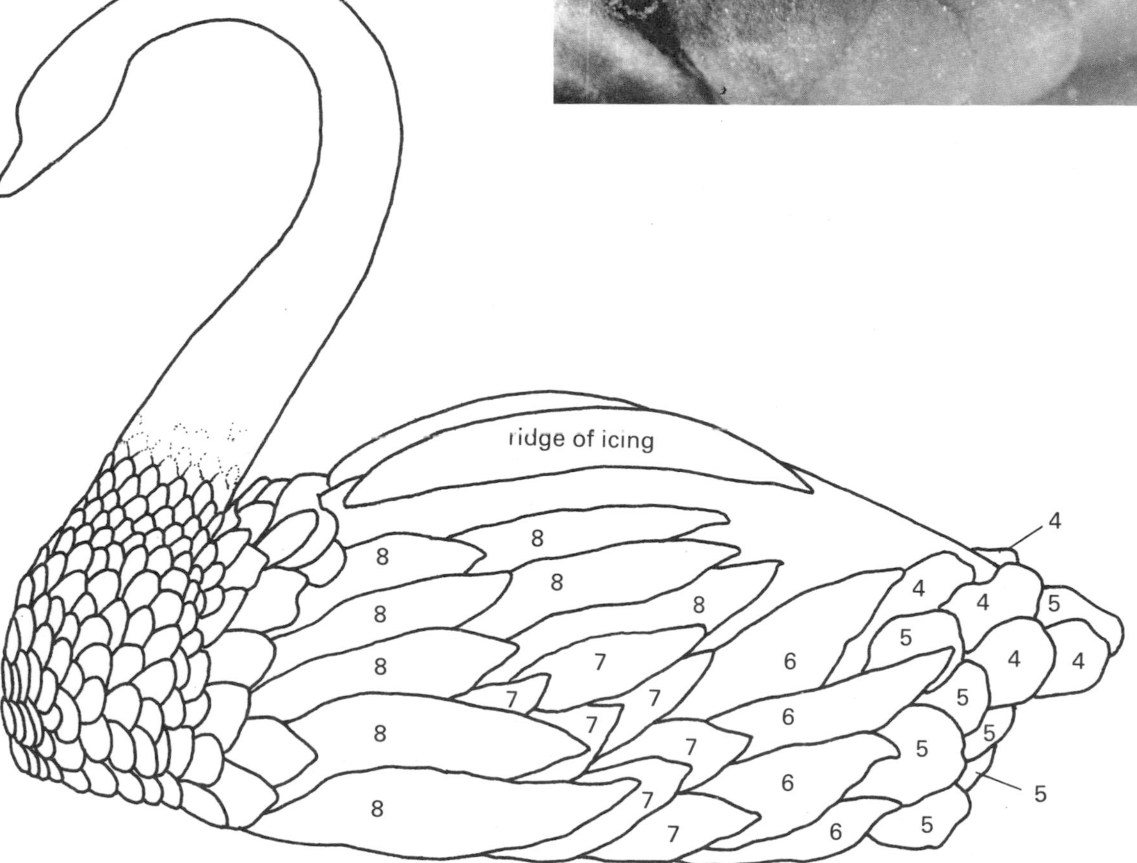

9 Cut out another number 5 feather. Flute its edges and moisten it. Place it on the underside of the tail, in the centre. The fluted top of the feather faces to the rear of the bird.

10 Cut out six more number 5 feathers. Flute their edges and moisten them. Place them in a line at the base of the bird's body at the rear, on either side of the swan. Working from the rear, place three feathers on the left side of the bird, then three on the right. Make sure they overlap a little.

11 Cut out another six number 5 feathers. Flute and moisten them. Place three in a wedge on one side of the swan, above the rear base feathers just added. Place a wedge of the other three on the other side of the bird. When both sets are in place there should be a space left across the tail of the swan at its body end.

12 Use the number 4 cutter to cut out three more tail feathers. Flute them, moisten their bases and place them across the top of the tail in the central space formed in Step 11.

13 To complete the rear and tail section of the swan use the number 4 cutter again to cut out two more feathers. Flute and moisten them. Place them higher up the tail (that is, at the body end), in front of the three feathers added in Step 12.

14 To begin to construct the sides of the swan cut out four pointed feathers, 7 cm long by 2 cm wide, using the number 6 cutter. Flute their top edges, moisten their backs and position them to the back of the right side of the swan. Place the first lengthwise at the base of the side, then another two in ascending order above it. The fourth feather is placed between the first two. Allow some of the frilled tips to sit out from the side of the swan.

Position four pointed feathers in the same way on the left side of the swan.

15 Using a long orchid cutter or the number 7 cutter, cut out seven more side feathers. Flute their edges, moisten their backs and place them on the right side of the swan to the front of the side feathers already in position. The first three are placed closely together in a vertical row, starting at the base of the cake; their tops overlap

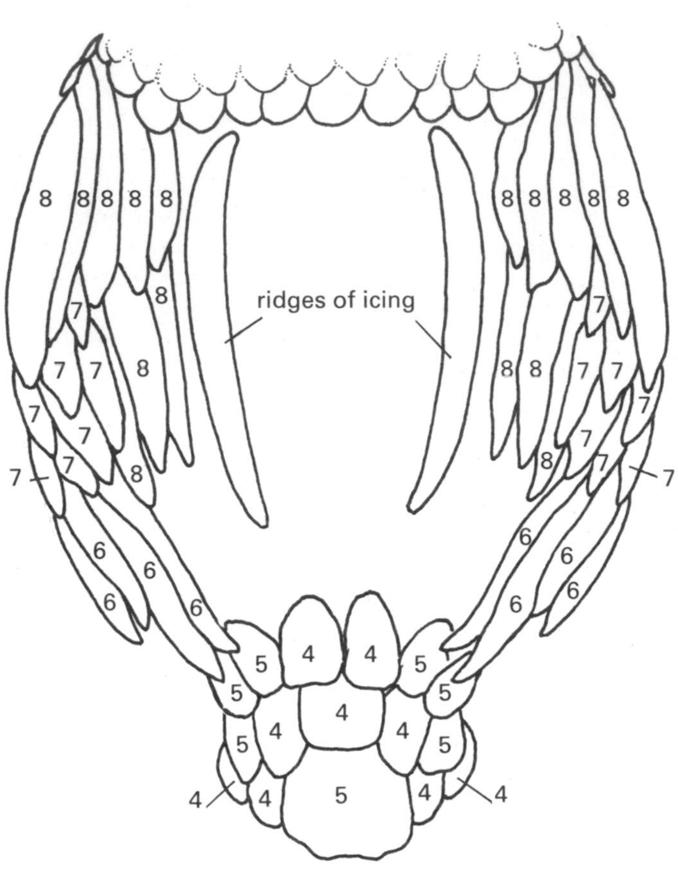

the base ends of the previously added side feathers. The next row of three is placed more diagonally so that the top of the base one lies between the first two feathers of the first row, and so on. The seventh feather is placed over the top feather in the first row and behind the top feather of the second row. Much more of this feather than of the others shows.

Assemble another seven feathers in the same way on the left-hand side of the bird.

16 Cut out another eight long, pointed feathers, using the number 8 cutter. Place three of these, lying lengthwise, in a vertical row on the swan's right side, higher up the side than the previously added number 7 feathers. The remaining five feathers are placed, one above the other, so that their tips partly overlap the first three number 8 feathers and the nearest number 7 feathers and their bases almost reach the small feathers that have already been positioned – ultimately their

bases will be covered when the last ruff feathers are added.

Position eight more number 8 feathers in the same way on the left-hand side of the swan.

17 The last work is to fill in the roughly heart-shaped space on the top of the cake, which forms the bird's broad back. This area includes the two ridges of soft icing added to accentuate the heart shape.

Cover the area with large feathers made by using cutters numbers 9, 10 and 11. The feathers need to be fluted to emphasise the frilly appearance of the folded wings. Moisten the backs of the fluted feathers and place them lengthwise on the bird. Naturally, the longest feathers should be used where the greatest space has to be covered. Make sure you place frilly feathers along the tops of the ridges to accentuate the height of the cake and to enhance the heart shape.

18 When the last section of the bird is complete, add more ruff feathers, if they are needed.

19 Add the plumage of the black swan to the second cake in the way that you have for the white swan, repeating steps 3–18.

Heads and Eyes

The heads and eyes of the swans are made more realistic by the addition of some red icing.

1 Colour some soft icing red. Knead a little in your hands, then roll it out into a very small piece. Moisten the beak area on the white bird. Cut a small V from the red icing, then place it so that the base of the V is located at the centre front of the beak. Press gently on the icing to make it adhere to the bird's beak. Use a scalpel to cut away any excess icing. The red icing sweeps to the sides of the beak, terminating in points at the eyes.

2 Moisten one side of two very tiny balls of red icing. Place them on the sides of the head just above the points of the red beak constructed in Step 1. Insert the tip of a skewer in the centres of the balls to create realistic-looking eyes.

3 Repeat Steps 1–2 for the black swan.

When the icing has dried completely, brush dry cornflour on the white swan and black petal dust on the black swan to give the pair a velvety appearance.

See colour plate

on page 71

Miniature Garden Cake

Gardens are wonderful places for peace, adventure, inspiration and relaxation. A cake in the form of a miniature garden can be enjoyed by all age groups. It also has unlimited potential because it is suitable for all sorts of occasions.

The Miniature Garden Cake has an air of mystery and rampant growth. This effect relies on the use of a multitude of different floral textures and shapes, rather than on the realistic depiction of particular flora. Known flora, like the wattle, is often presented in unusual ways, and all vegetation is kept low so that the garden tumbles gracefully down to the pool. The Miniature Garden Cake shown in the colour plate offers many suggestions for flower and leaf designs, but it need not be a blueprint. Choose your favourite flowers and adapt the instructions given below to your own uses; however, make sure you create a sense of variety and abundance – and a touch of fantasy.

The Miniature Garden Cake illustrated is made from a fruit cake mixture (see Recipes chapter) and covered with bought almond and soft icings. Because the cake offers great scope for intricate and time-consuming decoration, it is best to use traditional cake recipes and icings so that nothing will spoil during the lengthy decorating process. Making a cake with a longer life also gives the many garden lovers you know more time in which to admire your creation!

The Miniature Garden Cake illustrated required one quantity of cake mixture (250 g butter) and 1 kg of soft icing for the covering.

Shaping the Cake

1 Use a regular 20-cm round cake tin for baking. Do not fill the tin too high, because additional height is gained when you come to make the top step, and you will lose the effect of a gently sloping garden if your cake is too tall. Once the cake has been cooked and cooled, remove it from the tin.

The three broad steps shown in the colour plate are made first to ensure that the cake is not dominated by the pool, which should really be quite small. The top step is built above the top of the cake after the other two have been made. The tread of the middle step is level with the cake top.

2 To form the side of the middle step and the tread of the bottom step cut a small, shallow wedge (allowing for the width of the step) out of the cake. Reserve the piece for construction of the top step.

3 Cut out another wedge to form the side of the bottom step and a small open space extending beyond the steps. Ensure the side of the bottom step is the same as that of the middle step, but make the open space more extensive than the tread of the middle step.

4 Use the wedge cut to form the middle step and some almond icing to build the top step, ensuring that its tread and side have the same dimensions as those of the other two steps.

5 Using more almond icing, build a slope, descending from the top step to the open space at the bottom of the steps, between the steps and the pool area.

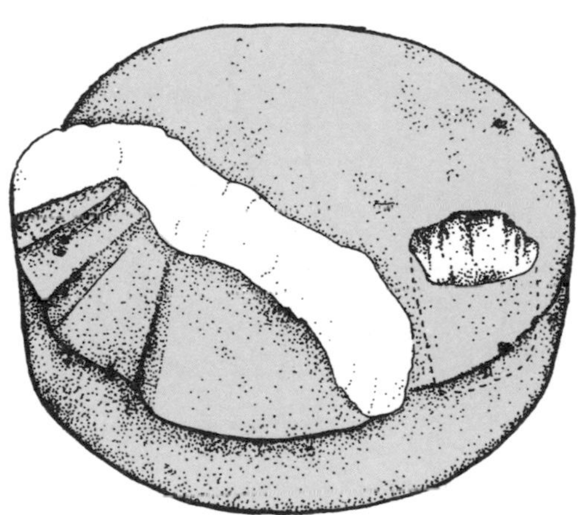

6 To make the pool, scoop out a small section (about a soupspoonful) of cake to the right of the slope. The base of the pool, which will later be covered with a thin layer of piping jelly to suggest water, is level with the open space at the foot of the steps.

Use a little more almond icing, if need be, to ensure that all the terrain has soft, gentle slopes and curves.

Covering the Cake

The cake is covered in the same way as a regularly shaped cake (see the chapter on Covering the Cake for instructions). The elasticity of the almond and soft icings ensures that all ridges and depressions are covered smoothly. Just ease the icing over any unusual formations. Allow the first (almond) covering to dry for 3–7 days before applying the final (soft icing) covering. Note that it will be easier to decorate the cake if the soft icing is coloured green. The cake can be placed on your presentation board before or after you have covered it, but it must be positioned before decoration begins.

The decoration of the cake involves forming the low-lying features, such as the water in the pool and the piped lily pads, leaves and grasses, first (Stage 1). The taller vegetation is then made and added to the cake (Stage 2). You may, however, need to make the toadstools described at the start of Stage 2 before you begin Stage 1, because they take a while to dry.

Decorating the Cake: Stage 1

The ground-plan provided shows you where the piped-on and ground-level features are placed. The plan is only an approximate one, and, of course, you are free to experiment with the placing of the Stage 1 decoration.

Water

1 The pool's base is covered with a small quantity of coloured bought or made (see Recipes chapter) piping jelly to look like the water's surface. Colour 1 tablespoon of piping jelly with some blue food colouring and stir it well. Spoon some of the jelly over the pool's base.

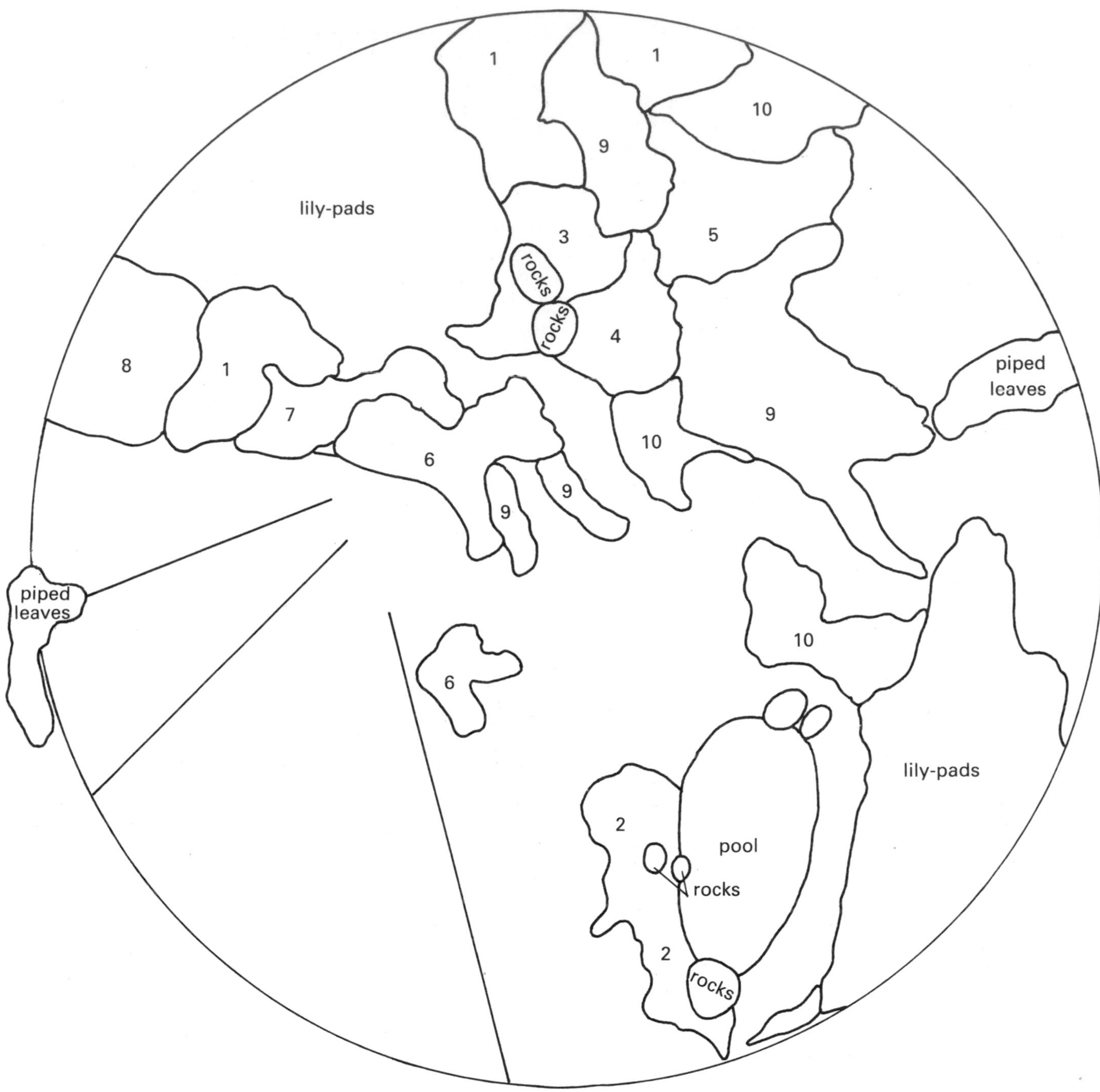

Stage 1 ground-plan

2 Use a paintbrush to form cascading water down parts of the pool's sides. Ensure the jelly is thin and varies in width to look like realistic trickles and runs of water. Work by drawing the jelly up to the top of the pool with the brush, so that you have more control of the flow of jelly. Vegetation can be used at the top of the sides to camouflage the ends of jelly.

Lily-pads

1 Colour two small amounts of soft-peak royal icing (see Recipes chapter) in different tones of green.

2 To ensure that all the lily-pads are uniform in size, use a sheet of graph paper on which a leaf pattern has been duplicated several times. Place the graph paper, then a sheet of waxed paper, on a thick piece of cardboard or Cane-ite board. Pin the papers down with drawing pins so that you have a firm working surface.

3 Using a paintbrush, brush plenty of royal icing onto each pattern. Make sure each lily-pad is convex and shiny. The darker icing should be placed to the left side of each leaf and the lighter to the right. Work down the waxed paper until you have made about fifty lily-pads. Set them aside to dry thoroughly, before placing them on the cake.

4 Once the pieces are dry, peel each off the waxed paper, brush its back with a little royal icing and place it on the cake.

The lily-pads in the illustration have been placed on the slope to the right of the pool, and just above the top step. Place them as naturally as possible, allowing them to curve and sweep so that other foliage can be merged with them.

Piped Grasses and Leaves

Several areas on the cake have been piped with royal icing to suggest grasses and tiny leaves. Several piping techniques are used to create variety in this low-lying vegetation. The numbers on the ground plan for Stage 1 broadly indicate where the following grasses and small leaves were piped on the Miniature Garden Cake:

1 small rounded dots in light green soft-peak royal icing
2 small peaked dots in light green soft-peak royal icing
3 small peaked dots in a darker green soft-peak royal icing than 1 and 2
4 medium peaked dots in darker green medium-peak royal icing
5 medium peaked dots in light green medium-peak royal icing
6 small leaves in darker green soft-peak royal icing
7 long peak lines in light green medium-peak royal icing
8 long peak lines in darker green medium-peak royal icing
9 small, short piped leaves in light green medium-peak royal icing
10 small, short piped leaves in darker green firm-peak royal icing

All the listed grasses and leaves are piped with a paper-cone bag (see Equipment chapter) that does not have a piping tube attached. Instead, using a fine pair of scissors, a small hole is cut in the point if you are piping any of the grasses, or a small V is cut for any of the tiny leaves.

Rounded dots Place the point of the bag, from which a small hole has been cut, where a dot is to be piped. Press the bag to allow some icing to be released, then stop the pressure, but still keep the point of the bag in the dot that has been formed. Finally, pull the point away.

Peaked dots These are formed using the same method described for rounded dots; however, keep the pressure on as you lift the point of the bag away from the dot. The longer the pressure is left on the bag after the point is pulled away, the longer will be the peak.

Peaked lines These are formed using the same method described for peaked dots, but the pressure is maintained on the bag for a longer period to ensure that a longer peak is formed.

Piped leaves Fill a paper-cone bag with royal icing coloured green, then flatten the tip of the bag and cut out the small V used for leaves. Press on the bag to release the icing and use a backwards and forwards pulling motion as you pipe, so that leaves are formed. Keep the pressure on the bag until just before you have completed the leaf, then release it and pull the bag back and away to form the final point.

Leaves have been piped in downward clusters on the left of the steps. A few similar but shorter leaves have been piped to the right of the steps in the centre of the slope. More of these leaves may be piped on the cake as required. They can also be used to keep clusters of flowers in place, when these are arranged later.

Decorating the Cake: Stage 2

The second ground-plan provided indicates where the taller vegetation was placed on the cake illustrated, once Stage 1 was completed. The vegetation used consisted of toadstools of varying heights, different ferns, grains, a variety of flowers and heart-shaped and longer leaves. In addition, piped drag leaves (see following instructions) were often employed to give the flowers a more realistic appearance.

Ferns can be any shape or length but they are always piped onto wire. Use several greens to add subtlety and variation.

All the flowers shown are small and short stemmed so that they blend harmoniously with the rest of the landscape. However, as long as you make sure you use a variety of flowers, you

Stage 2 ground-plan

can substitute your favourites for those shown.

Again, the ground-plan only shows approximately where the vegetation has been placed on the cake illustrated, and you should feel free to experiment with the design of your own cake.

Drag Leaves

Fill a paper-cone bag with green soft icing. Cut a small hole at the tip and commence piping. Press the bag until a dot is formed. Keeping the pressure on, pull the point of the bag along until the required length has been achieved. Stop pressing and drag the tip of the bag away.

Toadstools

1 Make a small hook at one end of nine 3–4-cm lengths of medium silk-covered wire.

2 Work up a small quantity of gum paste (see Recipes chapter) and colour it beige. The paste is of a suitable consistency when enough cornflour has been added to make it soft and pliable, but firm enough not to stick to the fingers.

3 Moisten all the wires, then roll some paste around them. Do not add too much paste, because the wires are to represent stems.

4 Mould a very small piece of paste to a small cup shape, using the handle of a paintbrush. Moisten the centre of the cap, then attach it to a paste-covered stem. Press and shape the paste again to ensure the shape looks like a very small baby toadstool. Repeat the process until six toadstools of graded sizes have been made. Place them in a bowl of cornflour so they will not distort as they dry.

5 The remaining stems are used for three larger, but graded, toadstools. Roll a small piece of gum paste into a ball. Press and flatten this a little between your fingers to form a toadstool cap. Use a pair of tweezers to make a series of thin lines around the underside of the cap. Moisten the centre and insert a stem into this. Turn the toadstool right side up and smooth and reshape it as required. Make the last two toadstools in the same way, then place all three on a bed of cornflour to dry.

6 When all the toadstools are completely dry, they may be placed in small clusters at the edges of the steps. Their colour may be adjusted by brushing their tops with a little methylated spirits and brown food colouring.

7 Pipe a few very fine, short lines of green-coloured royal icing on the cake, using a paper-cone bag with a small, cut hole or a number 00 tube, to represent short grass growing between the toadstools.

Long Ferns

1 Place several pieces of moistened, medium silk-covered wire on small individual pieces of waxed paper. Pipe a long, fat strand of green soft-peak royal icing along the top 2–3 cm of each wire, using a paper-cone bag with a small, cut hole or a number 00 tube. Fold the waxed papers over the icing, then gently press down a little so that the icing is flattened.

2 Set the wires aside to dry before peeling them off the waxed paper.

3 Assemble the fern stems in clusters so they look like a small bush. Insert the short stems of the clusters into the cake covering and pipe some small drag leaves at their bases to ensure they are all held firmly in place.

Round Ferns

1 Short, rounded stems of fern are made using the method described for long ferns, except that, instead of piping a long strand, short, fat, green dots are piped at intervals along each stem, using a paper-cone bag with a small, cut hole or a number 00 tube.

2 Assemble the short ferns as you did the long.

Herring-bone Ferns

1 Place several short strands of moistened, medium silk-covered wire on small individual pieces of waxed paper. Pipe a series of small, green drag leaves (see above) along each wire. These are set at a 45-degree angle to the wire and arranged in pairs on either side.

2 Set the piped wires aside to dry.

3 Peel off the paper and turn each stem over. Pipe another series of leaves over the top of the previous leaves so that you produce a double-sided fern stem.

4 When the second sides are dry, attach the stems to the cake as you did the long fern leaves.

Fine Ferns

1 Place several short stems of wire on separate pieces of waxed paper. Pipe a series of small dots along the top of each wire, using a paper-cone bag with a small, cut hole or a number 00 tube.

2 Set each stem aside to dry.

3 Turn the wires over and pipe another series of dots on their backs.

4 When the second sides are dry, attach the stems to the cake as you did the long fern leaves.

Wattle

1 Use several short pieces of medium silk-covered wire as stems. Place a short wire against each stem so that it forms a T. Twist the short wire around the stem a few times to attach it firmly. Repeat the procedure until each stem has two or three small wires attached.

2 Attach a small piece of gum paste to each wire end, then work it into a shape that resembles a wattle ball. Pinch and squeeze the paste so that it will remain attached securely.

3 Set the wires aside to dry thoroughly before colouring.

4 When the balls are dry, pull the cross-wires up the stems to create a fuller effect.

5 Colour the balls with a little lemon colouring added to methylated spirits. Roll them in some sugar before they dry, so that the crystals attach themselves.

6 Set the balls aside to dry again.

7 Insert each stem in the cake. Pipe a series of small drag leaves (see above) at the base of the wires to secure them.

Ears of Corn

1 Cut off the tips of several stamens at both ends. Attach a small piece of gum paste at one end of each stamen. Ensure the paste remains oval in shape and that a short end of cotton protrudes beyond the paste. Press and squeeze the paste to make sure it is attached firmly. Using the blade of a pair of scissors, make a short line in the paste of each ear, along its length.

2 Set the ears of corn aside to dry, then colour them pale gold with a little colouring added to methylated spirits.

3 Arrange the corn stalks in dense clusters so that they look very effective. Pipe a series of drag leaves (see above) on the cake, then set the clusters in these. If the cottons are too long they may need to be trimmed so that they will stand upright.

Oat Stalks

1 Take five short pieces of medium silk-covered wire. Attach to each of these a small piece of gum paste. Squeeze each piece to ensure that it is firmly secured, then press it into a piece of tulle so that a pattern is formed on its surface. Cut each piece into a small, triangular shape.

2 Set the oat stalks aside to dry, before colouring them a pale gold with a little colouring added to methylated spirits.

3 Attach the oat stalks to the cake by inserting the base of each stem in the cake covering.

Forget-me-nots

1 Forget-me-nots are easy to make, using a small cutter. Roll out a small piece of gum paste as thinly as possible, then cut out a flower.

2 Place the flower shape on a piece of foam. Press down on its centre, using the ball end of a curler pin. Insert the cut end of a stamen through the centre, then draw the flower up to the stamen head. Pipe a small dot of royal icing behind the stamen head to ensure the flower is firmly attached.

3 Set the forget-me-nots aside to dry before colouring.

To add variety, present the forget-me-nots in clusters of different colours, using a little colouring added to methylated spirits. Some can be altered further by pinching a point at the tip of each petal. Other flowers can be changed by cutting each petal a little deeper with a scalpel.

Pea Flowers

1 Make nine buds to go with the flowers, using short lengths of medium silk-covered wire. Place a small knob of gum paste on the end of each piece and shape it into a very small oval.

2 To make the pea flowers themselves, attach a small piece of paste to the end of several pieces of wire. Press a line down the centre of each piece of paste so that it looks as if it has been almost cut in half.

3 Take several more pieces of paste and press each between your fingers to form very small, round petals 5 mm in diameter. Mark and moisten a line down the middle of each petal. Place one centrepiece that you made in Step 2 along the line of each petal. Pinch and squeeze the bases of the flowers being formed so that the two sections of each join securely. Press the back of a scalpel blade into the top of each petal to form a small V.

4 Set the pea flowers and their buds aside to dry before colouring with a little mauve colouring added to methylated spirits. They were presented on the cake illustrated in a cluster of yellow and a cluster of mauve. The mauve pea flowers and buds were surrounded by short, heart-shaped leaves (see below).

Waxflowers

1 Make a small hook at one end of several short pieces of fine, medium cotton-covered wire, which will become the stems of the waxflowers and their buds.

2 Moisten the hooked end of two or three wires and attach a very small ball of gum paste to each. Press and squeeze the paste between your fingers to form small, oval waxflower buds. Set the buds aside to dry.

3 Shape a ball of paste into a small cone. Insert the handle of a paintbrush into the cone, then use a pressing motion to hollow out the cone. Turn the cone in your fingers as you press so that the edge is thinned evenly. Push the cut end of a moistened piece of wire through the hollowed cone and out its point. Pinch and squeeze the paste around the point to ensure it is attached securely to the hooked end of the wire.

4 Divide the hollowed cone into five equal sections, using a pair of fine scissors. Mitre the corners and shape the five petals a little. Pinch and squeeze the petals to give them a softly pointed finish. Insert five very short pieces of stamen cotton into the centre of the flower and dust the stamens with yellow petal dust.

5 Make four more waxflowers in the manner described in Steps 3 and 4 and set them aside to dry.

6 Assemble the flowers and buds in a small cluster as shown in the colour plate and plan. Insert the cluster in a bed of piped drag leaves (see above), so that they remain firmly in place.

Gypsophila

1 Make a small hook at one end of several short pieces of medium silk-covered wire.

2 Squeeze a small ball of gum paste between your fingers to form a thin, circular piece. Place it on a hard part of your hand and flute its entire edge by rolling the end of a cocktail stick backwards and forwards along it. This motion thins and enlarges the outer area of the circle so that it increases in diameter and then curls.

3 Fold the piece of paste in four to give it a wedge-like shape. Roll the point of the wedge onto the moistened hooked end of a piece of wire, then pinch and squeeze it to secure it firmly.

4 Make four or five of these white flowers and assemble them on the cake in the way that you did the waxflowers.

Daisies

1 Roll a small quantity of gum paste between your fingers to form a very tiny, pointed sausage about 1 cm in length.

2 Use a cocktail stick to thin and curl the length of the sausage by placing the stick along the length of the paste, then rolling it from left to right. Curl both ends up a little.

3 Make several white petals in the same way, then set them aside to dry.

4 Pipe a series of medium peaked dots on the cake and set the petals in these, allowing five petals per daisy.

Irish Heath

1 Make a small hook at one end of several short pieces of fine cotton-covered wire.

2 Make heath buds by adding a small piece of gum paste to the moistened, hooked end of four wires. Press and squeeze the paste until a long, pointed bud has been formed on each wire. Use a fine pair of scissors to cut into the body of each bud: make five incisions around the base of each so that very finely pointed sepals are formed. The sepals must remain attached to each bud.

3 Make a heath flower by inserting the moistened hooked end of a piece of wire into a small ball of gum paste. Pinch and squeeze the base of the paste so that it is attached firmly to the wire. Insert the ball end of a curler pin into the top of the paste and shape the paste into a ball that is fat at the base and narrower at the top. Pull the curler pin out of the flower, then reshape the top so that it remains narrow. Use a fine pair of scissors to make sepals in the same way that you did those of the buds.

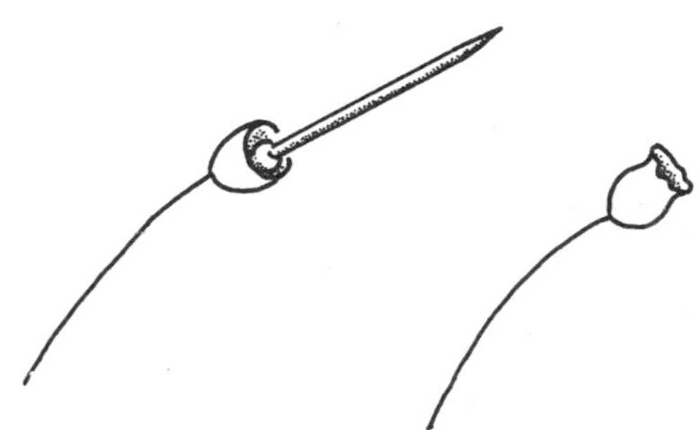

4 Make six more flowers, following Step 3, and set them aside to dry.

5 The sepals of the white heath are coloured green: use a little food colouring diluted with a little methylated spirits. Set the flowers aside to dry again.

6 Assemble the flowers and buds in a small cluster as indicated in the colour plate and plan.

Snowdrops

1 Remove the tips from several stamen cottons. Moisten one end of three of these and attach a very tiny piece of gum paste to each. Press and squeeze each piece of paste to form a small snowdrop bud.

2 Attach a small piece of gum paste to one end of eight cottons to make the snowdrops. Press and squeeze the paste of each to attach it securely, then insert the tip of a cocktail stick into its centre. Push the cocktail stick gently so that a very small, hollow cup is formed, but be careful because these tiny flowers are very fragile.

3 Set the flowers and buds aside to dry before dusting them with a pale blue petal dust.

4 Arrange the flowers and buds in a cluster as indicated in the colour plate and plan.

Short, Heart-shaped Leaves

1 Make a small hook at one end of several pieces of medium silk-covered wire.

2 Moisten the hooked end of each, then press a small piece of gum paste onto it. Squeeze and flatten each piece of paste between your fingers so that it becomes thin. Use a pair of scissors to cut a heart shape in each and remove the excess paste. Mark a central vein in the leaves, then curve each under a little. Make the leaves in graded sizes.

3 Colour the leaves with some green food colouring diluted with methylated spirits. Different combinations of green, yellow and brown will achieve different greens.

4 The heart-shaped leaves were assembled on the cake illustrated with the mauve pea flowers.

Long, Narrow Leaves

1 Form these in the way that you did the heart-shaped leaves; however, make them longer and narrower and curve the sides inwards a little.

2 Colour the leaves as described in Step 3 for the heart-shaped leaves.

3 The long, narrow leaves were assembled in a cluster at the edge of the cake illustrated, on the top step.

Finishing Touches

Some very small pieces of sugar rock were also on the cake illustrated. To make sugar rocks see the instructions given for the Castle Cake.

A final colouring will give the garden a soft and mellow appearance. Paint over some of the cake's surface, including the various grasses, leaves and rocks, so that everything appears to have light and dark shades. Use a combination of dry green, brown and black petal dust applied with a large, soft sable paintbrush.

Pipe a series of small drag leaves (see above) at the base of the cake to complete the decoration. Use a royal icing coloured one shade darker than the cake covering.

Miniature Garden Cake

(see page 60)

Noah's Ark Cake

See colour plate

on page 72

Noah's Ark Cake

This is a wonderful cake for young and old alike. Whether for a birthday or just a light-hearted celebration, it has lots of appeal. It needs to be positioned with both sides visible so that all the animals can be fully appreciated.

Use the colour plate, which shows both sides of the Noah's Ark Cake, as a guide when you model the animals. You may wish to include animals not shown in the illustration – adapt the instructions for making particular animals to your own requirements. The more animals that can be accommodated on the ark, the merrier.

Note the interest of the cake is created by the arrangement of the different shapes, sizes and colours of the animals, and that much of the humour comes from the juxtapositioning of unlikely shipmates: crocodiles and snakes would hardly be the most comfortable companions on board such a crowded vessel. The expressions on the animals' faces also add to the liveliness of the cake.

A fruit cake must be used for the Noah's Ark Cake so that the weight of the animals does not sink the ship. The cake illustrated required one quantity of cake mixture (250 g butter) and 1 kg of bought soft icing for the covering. In addition, 1.8–2 kg of soft icing was required for moulding the animals.

Shaping the Cake

1 Bake your fruit cake (see Recipes chapter) in a 20-cm, ovenproof basin or mixing bowl to achieve the ark's shape.

2 Once the cake has cooled remove it from the bowl. To make the ark cut away the cake on either side of a central oblong piece 10–12 cm wide. Reserve the two side sections for the top of the ark.

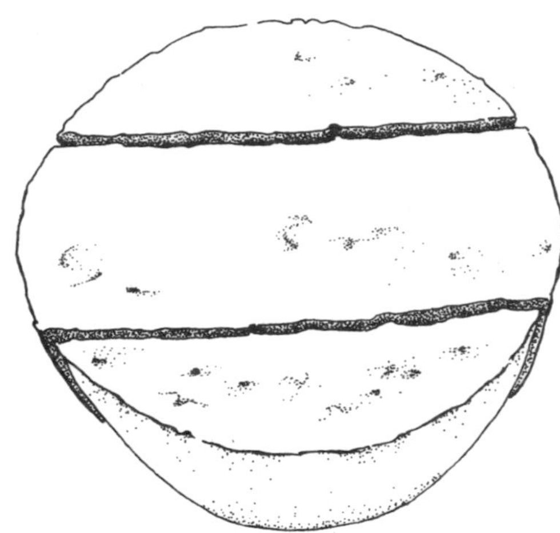

3 Fill any holes on the cut sides of the oblong piece with bought almond icing. Insert several bamboo skewers in the cake at both ends. Using more almond icing, build up the ends of the ark to look like the stern and the prow. Ensure that the skewers are encased within the icing. The front of the ship is more pointed than the rear.

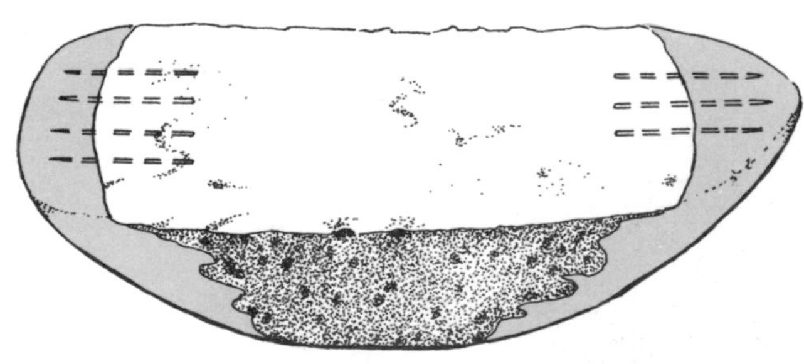

4 Skewer the two leftover pieces of cake together and cut their sides to create a rectangular cabin for the ark. Make sure it is correctly proportioned for your ark. Insert bamboo skewers in the top surface of the ark to secure the cabin. Position the cabin towards the rear so that the front half of the ark is clear, but leave a little free space at the rear, also. The ark and its cabin look like a very simplified, toy boat at this stage, but they will look much more interesting when completed.

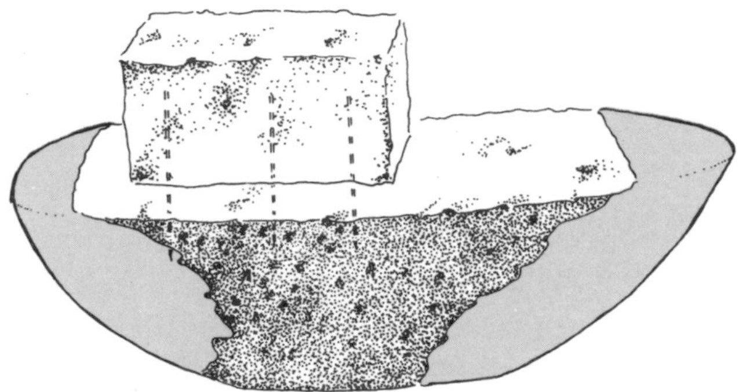

Covering the Cake

1 Glaze the cake with warmed apricot jam, then cover the entire cake with a thin layer of almond icing (see the chapter on Covering the Cake).

2 Allow the almond icing to dry for a week to ensure it becomes firm, then glaze the surface with egg white. Cover the whole ship with a layer of brown-coloured soft icing (see the chapter on Covering the Cake).

3 Use a small bottle top or a small, round cutter to make six portholes in both sides of the ark.

4 Allow the icing to dry for a few days, then decorate the cake with the animals.

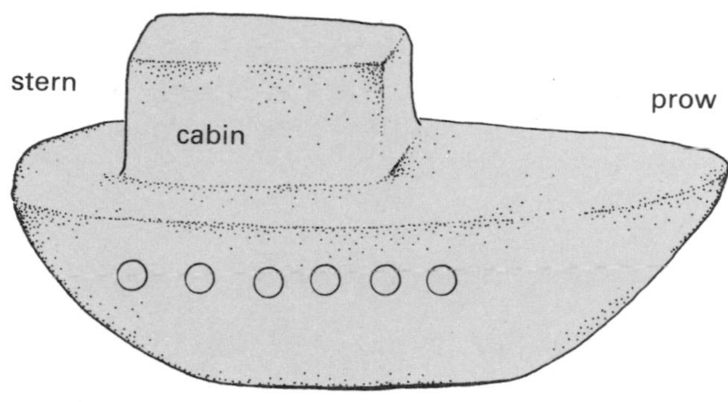

Animals

Naturally all the animals are made in pairs.

Start by colouring several amounts of soft icing in different colours with powdered food colourings. To make the animals shown in the colour plate, you will need icings coloured white, black, dark and light brown, light and dark grey, green, tan, beige, yellowish orange, pink and dusty yellow.

Make the large animals first, so that the smaller ones may be located in the spaces created between them. Use bamboo skewers to secure the large animals to the cake. The skewers are placed in the cake first, then the animals are pushed onto them. The skewers also ensure that the animals retain their poses. The skewers should not be too long for the heights of the animals. Some of the larger animals may need two skewers rather than one. The animals are not always made in complete detail; often just the upper part or the front legs are enough to suggest creatures in a crowded boat.

As you will notice in the colour plate, the elephants, giraffes, camels, skunks, rabbits, hedgehogs, pelicans, mice and one crocodile and one zebra face in the same direction, while the rest of the animals face the opposite way. Some of the animals are attached to the cabin, some to the deck (use the colour plate as a guide).

Side of ark facing rear

Elephants

1 Shape some dark grey soft icing into a squat, fat sausage. Make another, just a little shorter and thinner, for the second elephant. Using a pair of scissors, cut into the top halves of the sausages to begin to differentiate heads from the bodies, but be careful not to separate the parts completely.

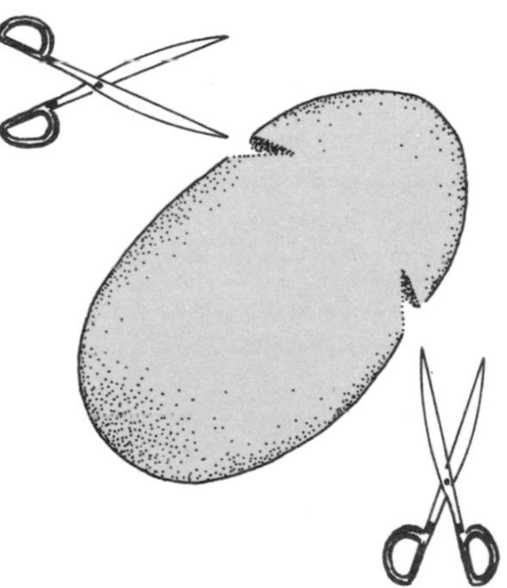

2 Pull and mould the top half of the sausages to form heads. Squeeze and pull the icing at the front of the heads to create trunks. Press the icing with your fingers to reshape the heads.

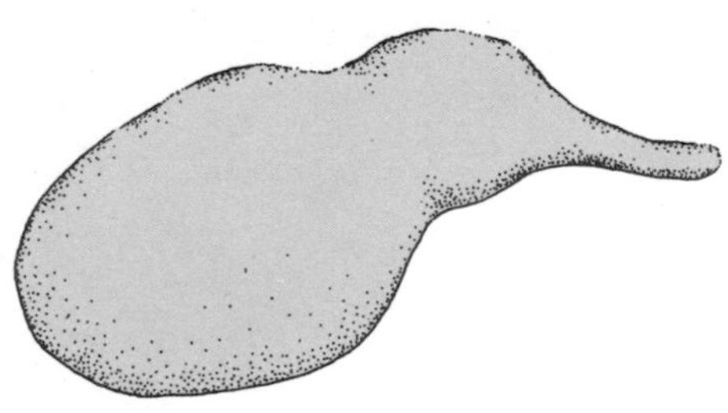

3 Use a small pair of scissors to cut ears on either side of the heads, being careful not to separate them from the heads completely. Mould and shape the ears, ensuring they stand out from the heads a little. Use a skewer to press a small, hollow opening in the tips of the trunks.

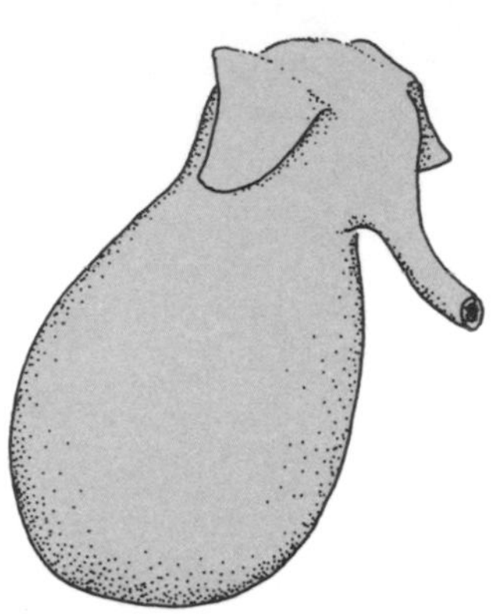

4 Make a small incision on each head for a mouth, with the small pair of scissors. The mouth of an elephant is under the trunk, quite close to the body. Make small depressions in the heads for eye sockets, then insert small pieces of black and white icing for eyes.

5 Moisten the bases of the elephants and push them onto the skewers that have been inserted in the top of the cake. Press and shape the animals to give them realistic poses.

Giraffes

1 Form two long, fat sausages from the yellowish orange soft icing. One sausage should be shorter than the other. Pull and squeeze the tops of both to shape heads. Pinch the ends of the heads to form snouts.

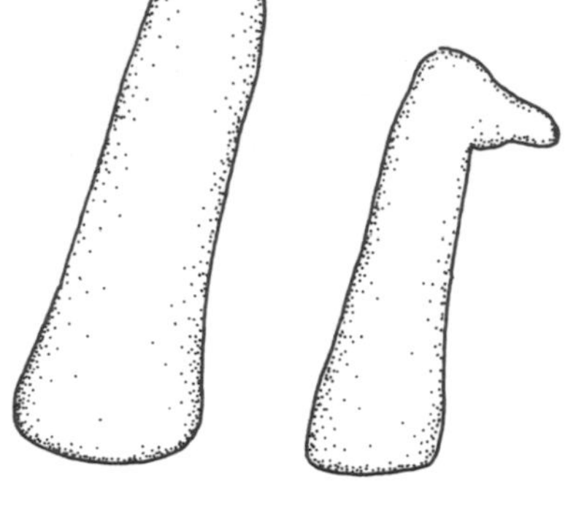

2 Pinch pairs of ears from the top parts of the giraffes' heads. Use a pair of scissors to cut out mouths. Make small, curved hollows in the ears, using a pottery tool (see Equipment chapter).

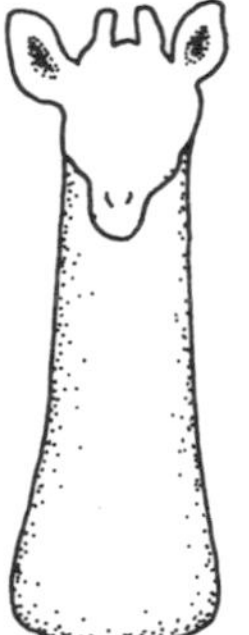

3 Moisten the bases of the giraffes, then push them onto the skewers that have been previously inserted in the cake. Ensure one giraffe is shorter than the other.

4 Press a pair of white eyes onto the faces of the giraffes. Add black paint to the centre of the eyes. Paint dark tan or brown patches all over the two bodies ensuring that these are smaller on the heads.

Camels

1 Shape the tan-coloured soft icing into two fat cones, one shorter than the other. Pull and press the top of each to shape the camels' heads, then slant these a little.

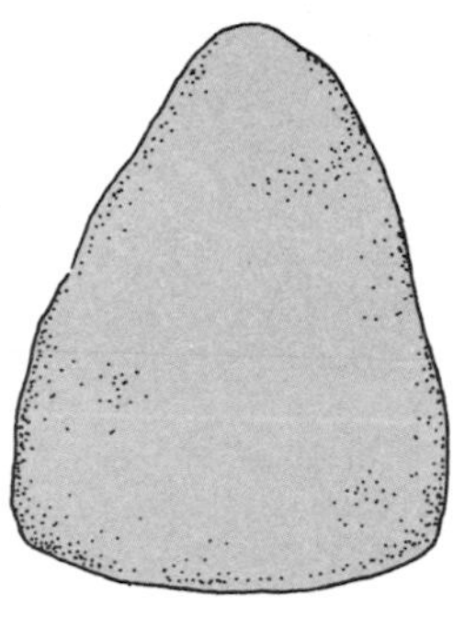

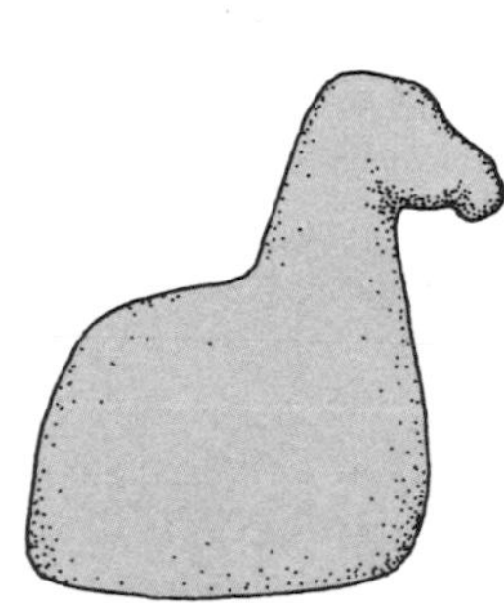

2 Press the back of the larger animal into a hump.

3 Squeeze out a pair of ears on the top of both heads. Use a pair of scissors to cut out mouths.

4 Moisten the bases of the animals, then position them on the skewers inserted in the cake. Ensure the heads continue to slant to give the animals a look of curiosity.

5 Make two small holes in both heads for the noses and press on some white and black icing to form eyes.

Zebras

1 Form two squat, fat footballs, one longer than the other, from some white soft icing.

2 Pull and press the footballs to form heads at the tops. Pinch out a pair of ears for each zebra and press small hollows in them, using a pottery tool. Ensure the heads have long snouts.

3 Pull out the icing to form a pair of legs at the front of both footballs, beneath the heads. The legs on the larger zebra should be a little longer than those of the small one.

4 Place a skewer in the front of the cake between a giraffe and a camel. Moisten the base of the small zebra and push it onto the skewer so that it faces the same way as the giraffe and camel. Mould it so that it leans on the camel (use the colour plate as a guide). The bulk of the small zebra's body cannot be seen from the side of the cake facing front because it is placed to the rear.

Place the larger zebra on the other side of the ark, with its back to the giraffes.

5 Use black food colouring to paint stripes on each animal, then eyes, noses and mouths.

Polar Bears

1 Mould light grey soft icing into two large footballs, one slightly bigger than the other.

2 Pull and pinch the top ends of the footballs to form heads. Pinch out a pair of ears on the top of each head. Make pointed snouts and slightly flatten the area above these.

3 Pull out two front legs from the main part of the smaller piece of icing, and four legs from the larger one.

4 Press a pair of white and black eyes onto each face.

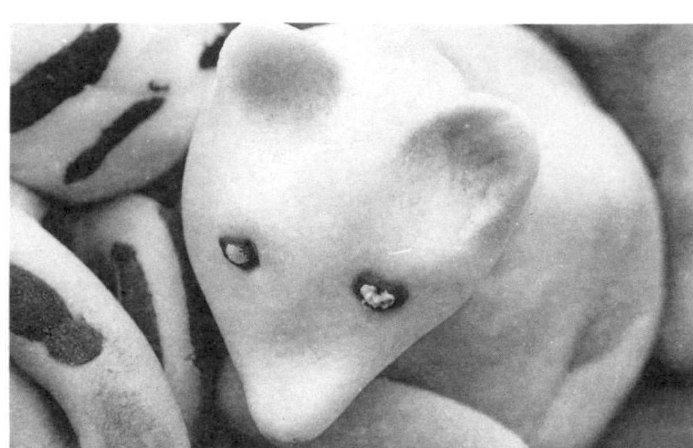

5 Moisten the bases of the bears. Push the animals onto skewers placed in the ark so that the smaller one is close to the prow of the ark and the larger bear is beside it to the rear. The smaller bear faces to the centre of the ark, with its back to the ship's prow. The larger bear is positioned close to the edge of the ark on the side facing away; it looks towards a crocodile. Place all the legs so they face to the front of the bodies. Press and slightly squeeze the backs of both bears to improve their shape.

Pigs

1 Mould pink soft icing into two small, fat footballs.

2 Pull out short, fat heads from one end of both footballs.

3 Use a pair of scissors to cut pairs of front legs from the bodies and also to cut small pairs of ears at the top of both heads.

4 Pull and pinch the snouts until you have achieved lifelike heads, then make indentations, representing a pair of eyes, for each pig. Colour in the eyes with a little black food colouring.

5 Moisten the bases of the pigs and position the animals on skewers in the cake behind the giraffes.

Leopards

1 Divide the dusty-yellow-coloured icing into two long footballs, one slightly longer than the other.

2 Pull out a long, tapering tail at one end of each, and squeeze and pinch the other end into a small cat face. The snouts are not as long as those on many of the other animals.

3 Pinch out a pair of ears on the top of each head. Press a pair of eyes made from dark brown icing on each of the faces. Do not worry about forming any legs on these cats.

4 Position the leopards to the rear side of the ark, one on top of the other and facing in opposite directions.

5 Paint blackish brown spots on the bodies of the leopards, using food colouring.

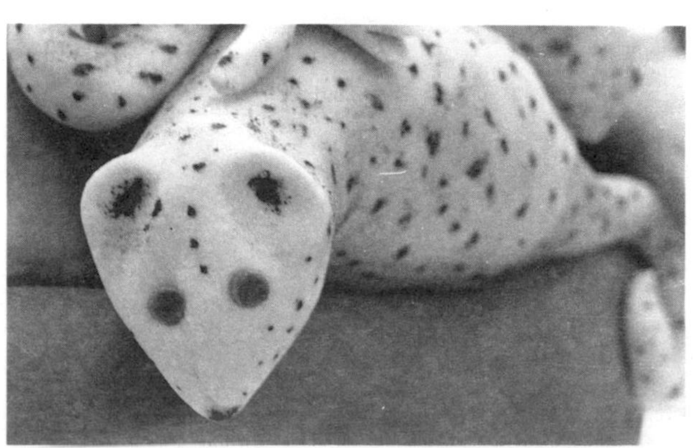

Crocodiles

1 Form two long, triangular shapes from some of the green soft icing. These will need to be rather fat to give the crocodiles their typical body shape. Shape the tapered end of both into a tail. Press and push the icing at the other end of both to form a head, then use a pair of scissors to cut out a long, deep mouth for each.

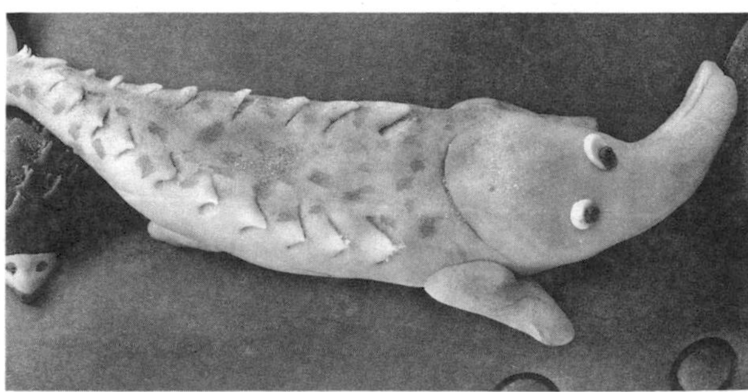

2 Use the pair of scissors to cut a pattern of scales on the bodies and tails of the crocodiles. The scales form one row on the tail, then divide to the left and right on the back.

3 Take a little more icing to form two legs for each crocodile. Moisten and then stick them onto the upper parts of the bodies. Press a pair of black and white eyes onto both heads.

4 Position a crocodile on either side of the top of the ark.

5 Paint hazy brown patches (see the colour plate) on the backs of both.

Skunks

1 Shape some dark brown soft icing into two sausages. Pull out the icing at one end of both sausages to form wide, fat tails. Pull and squeeze the other end of the sausages to form heads. Ensure the snouts are fine and pointed.

2 Pinch out four legs from the main body of one animal, but only the two front legs from the body of the other.

3 Smooth and flatten small pieces of white icing and moisten the backs of these. Place them on the animals to form the white markings seen in the colour plate. Press a pair of white eyes on each of the skunks.

4 These skunks are only small so they do not require skewer supports. Moisten their bases then position them between the elephants in suitable poses. The two-legged skunk is placed to the front, with the other above and behind it, as the colour plate shows.

Rabbits

1 Shape a small amount of beige-coloured soft icing into two small footballs. Pull and press the footballs to form two bodies with small heads and pointed snouts.

2 Use a pottery tool to pull up the icing into a pair of ears on each animal.

3 Squeeze out a pair of legs for the fronts of both.

4 Moisten the bases of the rabbits, then position them on the ark at the base of the giraffes.

5 Use a skewer to make noses and mouths in their faces.

Hedgehogs

1 Shape some dark brown soft icing into two balls.

2 Press pieces of beige soft icing onto the front of both balls and pull the pieces into pointed faces. Moisten some small, dark pieces of icing and press them onto the animals' faces to form their eyes and mouths.

3 Use a pair of scissors to make a series of incisions all over each body to create the effect of spikes.

4 Moisten the bases of both hedgehogs, then press them onto the ark against the camels.

Pelicans

1 Form two large birds with long necks from some white soft icing.

2 Attach some pink soft icing to the heads to create beaks.

3 Moisten one side of some small pieces of dark brown icing and press the pieces onto the rear ends and sides of the birds. Adjust the pieces so that they resemble the markings on pelicans.

4 Use a pair of scissors to cut wings on either side of the birds.

5 Paint a pair of black eyes on each bird's head.

6 Insert two short skewers into the larger elephant's head. Moisten the birds' bases and position them on the head of the elephant. Slant the beaks of each a little differently to give the pelicans character.

Mice

1 Form a small amount of beige soft icing into two very tiny, rather pointed footballs.

2 Pull out one end of each to create long, thin tails. Pinch the other ends of the two footballs to form pointed heads and faces.

3 Moisten the bases of the mice and position them on the side of the ark that faces front. One mouse is at the prow of the ark, next to the back of a polar bear, the other is on the other side of the same polar bear, next to a camel.

4 Make eyes, ears and mouths in the heads with a skewer.

Snakes

1 Divide green soft icing in two. Roll both pieces into medium sausages.

2 Press small pieces of brown icing along parts of the sausages to create the markings on the snakes' skins, then roll out the sausages to thin and lengthen them.

3 When the snakes are long enough, push the icing at one end to given them small, slightly pointed heads. Cut out mouths and make indentations for pairs of eyes, in the heads. Colour in the eyes with a little brown food colouring.

4 Position the snakes on the ark separately. One is located between the polar bears and giraffes, while the other is draped between the two pigs and partly over the leopards.

Finally, use some petal dust to highlight details on the animals.

See colour plate

on page 90

World Map Cake

A cake decorated with an old map of the world surrounded by sailing ships holds much appeal for many people. The World Map Cake shown in the colour plate, which displays a map drawn in 1700, can be used for birthdays or retirement parties or to wish someone *bon voyage* – the old-style ships suggesting the romance of travel. You can, of course, choose your own favourite map and other nautical details, using the techniques explained in the chapter to create your own unique work.

A fruit cake mixture (see Recipes chapter) was used for the cake illustrated. It required three quantities of mixture (750 g butter) and 2 kg of soft icing.

Shaping the Cake

The cake needs to be baked in a very large, rectangular tin so that it is a sufficient size to display the map and sailing ships properly. A baking dish 33 cm by 30 cm was used for the cake shown. Do not make too deep a cake: the paintings of ships should flow freely from the front side of the cake to the periphery of the top.

Covering the Cake

1 Cover the cake with bought almond icing first, then with soft icing, following the instructions given in the chapter on Covering the Cake.

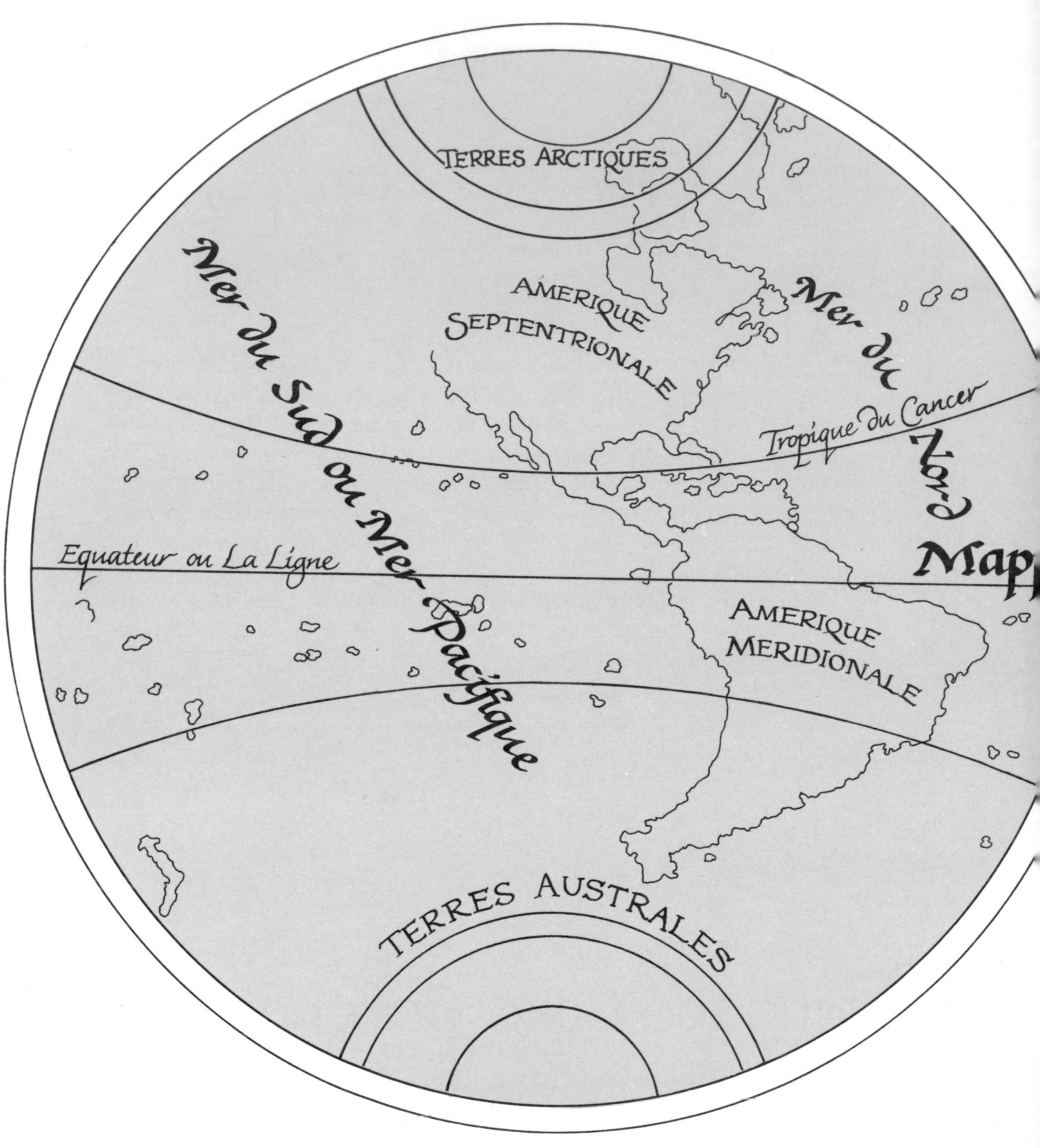

Pattern for map

Terres Arctiques
Mer Glaciale
Europe
Asie
Perse
Indes
Chine
Mer du Sud
Afrique
Arabie
Tropique du Capricorne
Nouvelle Hollande
Mer des Indes
Terres Australes

Pattern for scene at front

In addition to providing a hard surface for the line work, the two layers will ensure that the cake lasts and does not discolour, spoiling the effect of the painting.

The icing of the cake illustrated has been coloured a very soft ivory to simulate parchment. Use 1 drop of caramel liquid food colouring for every 500 g of icing used. Knead the icing well so that the colour spreads evenly.

2 Allow the final icing to dry for at least a week before commencing the painting.

3 Cover a suitably sized presentation board with gold foil, scrape some royal icing (see Recipes chapter) on it, then lift the cake onto it, using two heavy-duty cake slides. Once the cake has been positioned, place a scraper against the cake above the position of one cake slide. Press against the side of the cake with the scraper as you pull the cake slide out. Repeat the procedure to remove the second cake slide. The action ensures that the slides do not break and damage the icing on the sides of the cake.

Map and Ships

Tracing the Picture

1 Trace the copy of the map provided. The pattern is to scale for the cake illustrated, but you can enlarge or reduce it on a photocopier to suit the size of your cake. Use good-quality tracing paper, otherwise you will find it hard to distinguish the traced lines. Once the whole map has been traced, turn the paper over and redraw the lines. You should now have a double-sided tracing that includes the outside circles of the spheres.

2 Trace the drawing provided of the sailing ships scene and the smaller, impressionistic drawing of masts, used on the sides of the cake. Draw over their lines on the reverse side of the paper. If you prefer to use other vessels or something a little more modern take a tracing from an illustration or photograph.

3 Place the completed tracing of the map on the iced cake, using four pins to hold it in place.

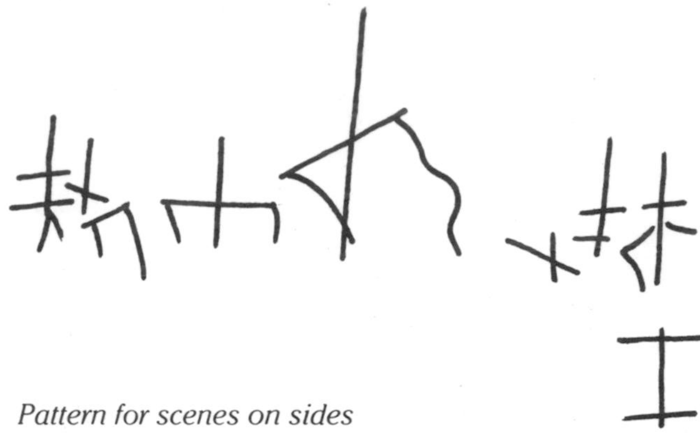

Pattern for scenes on sides

Be sure to put the pins in places where lines are to be drawn so that no holes are left on the surface when your work is completed.

Draw over the traced lines with a pencil, checking that you have followed every one. Remove any smudge marks by rubbing gently with day-old bread crumbs.

4 Place the sheet on which the ships have been traced over the cake, making sure the drawing lies beyond the outside circles of the map and curves down the front of the cake. Once again, use some pins to hold the drawing in place, then draw over the ships with a pencil. The finished decoration will be a little hazy to represent ships sailing on a misty sea, so your drawn lines do not have to be sharp. Repeat the procedure for the side illustrations.

Painting the Map

1 Mix together a few drops of black and sky blue colouring in a small, shallow, white dish so that it is possible to check the resulting navy blue. Add just a little brown, if necessary.

Two paintbrushes are used. A very fine, long-haired sable brush, similar to that used by china painters, gives excellent, controlled lines when you are painting the lines and circles of the map. Another sable brush, size 0 or 1, is useful for creating a shoreline effect along the coasts of the countries. Use a little methylated spirits on the brushes to spread the colouring easily. Sometimes the texture of icing causes neat colour to roll across the surface of a cake and fall in uneven streaks. Methylated spirits helps to overcome this problem.

2 The countries of the map are painted first, then the surrounding circles, lines and place names. Place a napkin under your hand when you work to protect areas already drawn and the clean icing surface.

The best results with the circles are achieved by painting in short, curving strokes that combined will make up a circle. Attempting the whole circle in a single sweep is more likely to result in an uneven, streaky outline.

The place names on the map should be painted in the same way as the circles. Alternatively, use a blue felt-tipped food pen.

Cocoa Painting the Ships

Cocoa painting achieves sepia-toned pictures that use the background colour of the cake covering to provide some of the highlights. Usually, cocoa painting involves the use of cocoa butter, cocoa and dark chocolate. Cocoa butter is the buff-coloured oil that remains after chocolate has been made; it is available from cake decoration stores and chemists. The ingredients for cocoa painting are usually added in equal proportions; however, if a heavier, chocolate-looking paint is required, more chocolate than cocoa butter should be used. For the World Map Cake only cocoa butter and white milk chocolate have been used. The blue and pale mauve or pink tones were achieved by adding a sprinkling of oil-based powdered colouring – chocolate can only be coloured using such special, oil-based powdered colourings.

This method of painting was chosen to provide softer areas of built-up paint than those achieved using floodwork. The blue and mauve tones accentuate the nautical theme and complement the outlines of the map.

1 Melt about 1 teaspoon each of white milk chocolate and cocoa butter in a small bain-marie or small bowl placed inside a larger bowl of hot water. (The small bowl will also act as a palette when you come to add colour to the chocolate–cocoa butter mixture.) The hot water under the bowl needs to be changed regularly so that the 'paint' remains at a spreading consistency.

2 Brush the combined white milk chocolate and cocoa butter over all the outer areas of the ships and sails, using a small, flat, 5-mm, short-haired sable paintbrush. Brush a much lighter covering over some of the inner areas. Once the coating has dried a little, you can begin to use the colours.

3 Using a satay skewer, place just a few grains of blue colour in a clean corner of the small bowl. Add to the chocolate–cocoa butter mixture a hint of blue, then brush the paint over the previously covered areas of the ships, creating areas of soft shade and deep highlights. If you make mistakes, you can scratch away the unwanted cocoa paint with a skewer.

4 Use a combination of blue colouring and cocoa butter only to paint in details on the ships, such as the masts and ropes. The long-haired or size 0 or 1 sable brushes, used for the map, are suitable for this work.

5 Once the ships have been completed, paint in the foreground and background. These areas are meant to be a very hazy swirl of blue, white and mauve. Paint them first with a very fine film of white milk chocolate and cocoa butter. Then place just a few grains of pink in a clean part of the small bowl and carefully mix a fraction with the chocolate–cocoa butter mixture to produce a very soft mauve. Brush a few hints of mauve shadow on the hazy areas. Use the colour plate as a guide.

6 Use the same cocoa painting technique to add the decorative details of impressionistic masts around the sides of the cake.

Shell Edge

To complete the cake a shell edge can be piped at the base, between the cake and the board.

1 Colour some firm-peak royal icing (see Recipes chapter) a pale blue. Fit a paper-cone bag (see Equipment chapter) with a number 8 star tube and fill it with the icing.

2 Hold the bag so that the tube is at a 45-degree angle to both the cake and the board. Press the bag so that icing is released and draw it along for about 1 cm. Allow the icing to build up a little at this point so that it forms a small bulge, then draw it along for another 1 cm. Continue in this way right around the cake. Merge any joins with a moistened paintbrush.

See colour plate on page 89

Grass Trees

Grass trees, or blackboys as they are sometimes known, can be found in many parts of Australia. They are a seemingly unusual subject for a cake, yet they can make ideal *bon voyage* or even anniversary cakes. The colour plate shows two grass tree cakes of different heights.

Because the cakes are very small it is best to use either a fruit cake mixture or a nutloaf recipe, and bake them in two cylindrical tins. Any empty coffee or processed vegetable cans are also suitable; however, try to use two tin cans that are different in width and height.

The Grass Trees illustrated required half a quantity of cake mixture (125 g butter) and 400 g of bought soft icing for covering them. An additional 600 g of soft icing was needed for the decoration.

Grass Trees

World Map Cake

(see page 81)

Shaping the Cakes

1 Choose a suitable cake mixture (see Recipes chapter). Grease the insides of the cake tins with a little oil, then sprinkle these areas lightly but thoroughly with plain flour. Add more cake mixture to one tin than the other, so that one grass tree will be taller. Once the cakes have cooled in their tins, loosen their sides by running a knife around them. The cakes should then slide out easily, after the tins have been tapped a little on the sides.

2 Use some bought almond icing to fill in and patch all the holes around the sides and tops of the cakes. Roll some more almond icing into short, fat sausages. Stick these on some sections of the cakes' sides. The bulges formed make the final cakes more like the real grass trees. It is also possible to give different slants to the cakes using this method.

In the first method, the icing is rolled out until it is as wide as the height of one cake and as long as the circumference. The cake is then rolled along this rectangle of icing and the join merged by rubbing it gently, with the hands. Lastly, a small circle of icing, of the same diameter as the cake, is rolled out and placed on top of the cake. The join is pressed and smoothed. The procedure is repeated for the second cake.

Alternatively, the measurement of one cake's height is doubled and added to that of the diameter. A circle of icing with a diameter of this measurement is rolled out, then placed over the top of the cake so that it falls evenly around the cake. The icing is smoothed against the surface of the cake by rubbing and pressing it gently with the hands. Any creases and folds are pressed downwards: work from the top to the bottom of the cake. In this way, excess icing is pushed onto the board. The icing is trimmed, if necessary. The procedure is repeated for the second cake.

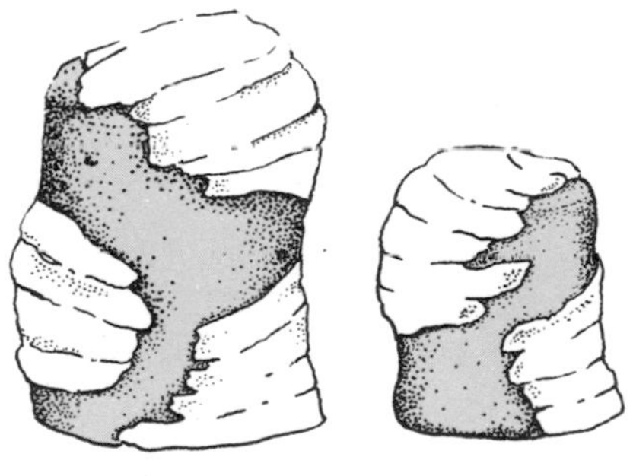

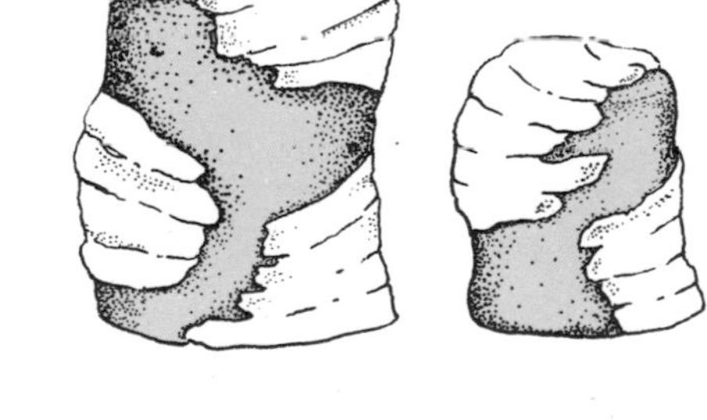

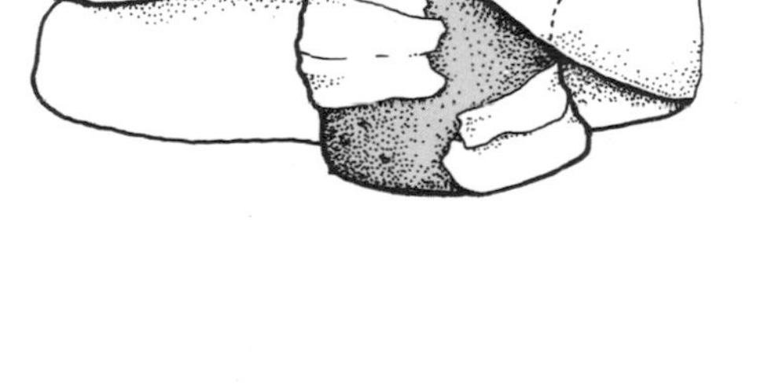

Covering the Cakes

1 Glaze all surfaces of both cakes, except the bases, with a little warmed apricot jam. Roll out some more almond icing, making sure it is large enough to cover the whole cake. Two methods can be used to cover the cakes.

2 Set the cakes aside to dry for a few days before glazing them with egg white and covering them with soft icing.

3 Colour soft icing a grey or grey-brown shade before applying it to the cake. Do this by kneading 2–5 drops of black or brown food colouring into the icing until evenly distributed.

4 Once the cakes have been covered with the soft icing, using either of the methods described in Step 1, make the patterns and creases illustrated, in their sides, with a skewer or a clean comb.

Do this before the icing becomes hard, then let the cakes stand for a week.

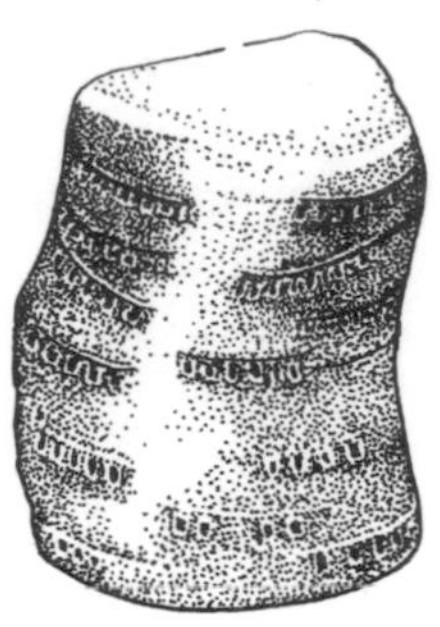

Adding Features

Leaves

1 Scrape a small amount of royal icing (see Recipes chapter) under both cakes and arrange them on a small, oval board. Use the colour plate as a guide.

2 Colour 200 g of soft icing dark grey, another 200 g pale green and a last 200 g dark green.

3 A garlic crusher, small spatula and long, thin satay stick are used for the following work. Press some of the grey icing through the crusher so that long strands of icing are formed. For longer strands, add more icing to the crusher as you work. You need to vary the length of the strands to give a natural appearance to the trees. Moisten the end of the small spatula and scrape the strands off the garlic crusher with it.

Use the satay stick to help position and press the strands onto the sides and tops of the cakes. The strands cover the top thirds of the trees. Work from the bottom of these areas to the top in a clockwise manner. The lower part of these areas has grey strands, while the rest has a combination of light and dark green icings, which have been pressed through the garlic crusher together to achieve a realistic effect.

4 The strands of icing at the very tops of the cakes need to be positioned carefully so that they do not become tangled. Use the other end of the satay stick to arrange the strands so that they look like the leaves of grass trees.

Flower Spikes

1 Take a piece of heavy cotton-covered wire, about 20–25 cm in length, and fold it in two. Moisten it with water, then roll some pale-lemon-coloured icing around it. Squeeze the icing until it becomes well attached. Press a little grey icing at the very base of the spike.

2 Roll the spike over a grater to give it indentations representing very small flowers. Trim the

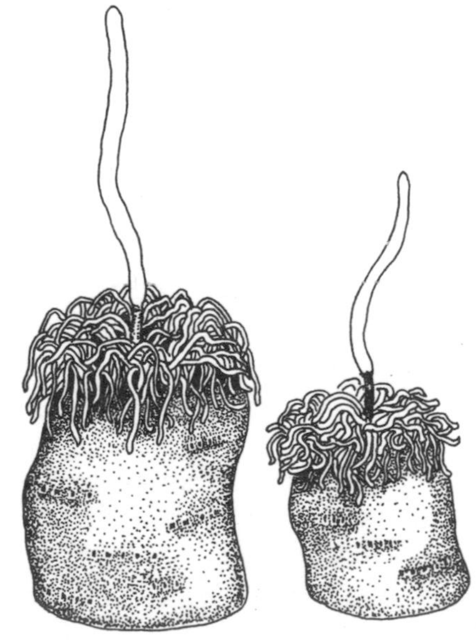

spike if necessary, then wrap the cut end with florists' tape. Insert that end into the centre top of one cake.

3 Repeat the procedure for the second cake, but be sure to make the spike of the taller cake higher than that of the small cake.

Finishing Touches

Rosella

1 Fill a paper-cone bag (see Equipment chapter) with a very small quantity of red soft-peak royal icing (see Recipes chapter). Cut a hole at the point of the bag, then pipe a large, rounded dot on the side of one spike; pipe another, smaller, peaked dot at the top of the first so that you now have a bird with a head (see the Miniature Garden Cake chapter for instructions, but note that, since you are piping a bird, the rounded dot and peaked dot will be larger than those used to suggest grasses and leaves).

2 Cut out two wings and two long tail feathers from small pieces of rice paper. Paint them blue, then set them in the royal icing body of the bird while it is still soft. The wings are placed on either side of the body. Pipe some more red soft-peak royal icing at the tail of the body to give it some length, then insert the feathers.

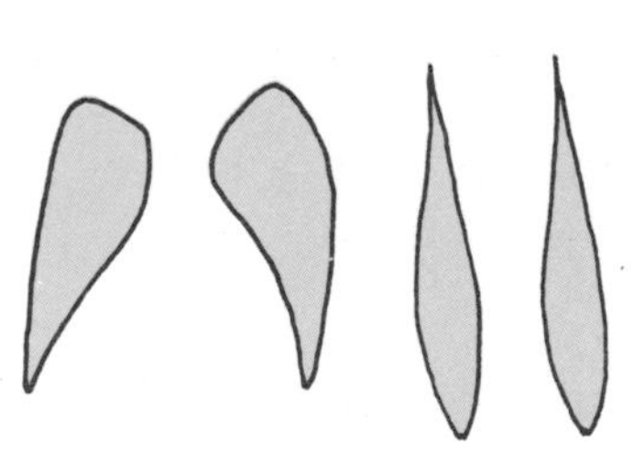

Grass

Pipe a series of small, medium and large blades of grass, in dark green soft-peak royal icing, around the bases of the cakes so that they cover a fair portion of the board. Make a paper-cone bag and cut a V at its point for this work. Use a forward and backward movement to pipe the blades and, if long, thin blades are being made, ensure the icing is still being pressed as the bag is pulled up and away. Be sure to vary the height and size of the blades of grass to add interest.

Colouring

Colour the sides of the trees with a little black petal dust, using a soft sable brush (see Equipment chapter). The colour should appear as uneven patches, because it represents the dark appearance the trees take on after bush fires. If some of the black falls here and there on the grass at the bases of the trees it will add to the effect.

The leaves on the tree tops can be dusted with a little green lustre powder to give them a soft, frosted look as well as to make them appear a little silvery.

See colour plate

on page 107

Anchor and Chain Cake

The Anchor and Chain Cake makes an ideal *bon voyage* cake or birthday or retirement cake for someone with nautical interests. The marzipan enthusiast will love this cake because the cake covering, shank and chain of the anchor can be made of bought marzipan. Only the arms of the anchor are cake. The sand is made of sugar and the shells and marine life are also moulded from sugar.

The cake illustrated has been made from a fruit cake mixture; however, the Anchor and Chain Cake may be made from any firm cake. If the cake is to be covered with marzipan only the one layer of icing is required. The cake requires one quantity of cake mixture (250 g butter) and 2 kg of bought soft icing or marzipan for the cake covering.

Shaping the Cake

1 Use one or two heavy-duty foil baking trays to make your cake tin. Press out all the folds of a tray so that you have as flat a piece of foil as possible. If it does not look big enough, cut a second flattened tray in half and staple each half at either end of the first tray.

2 Cut away a small, triangular piece from two diagonally opposite corners. Loosely fold the foil in half along the diagonal between the two remaining corners to form a canoe-like container.

3 Trim away any excess foil, then fold and press the foil at the two ends so that your cake mixture will not leak out during baking. The ends should be a little pointed to suggest the anchor's shape.

4 Any of the firmer cakes given in the Recipes chapter may be used; however, the decorating instructions that follow are for covering a fruit cake. Bake the cake in the foil shape, with a baking tray beneath it to catch any drips.

2 Select a suitable presentation board. Scrape a little royal icing (see Recipes chapter) under the base of the cake and place the cake on the board. Use more almond icing to build up the flukes on either arm of the anchor, as well as the crown between.

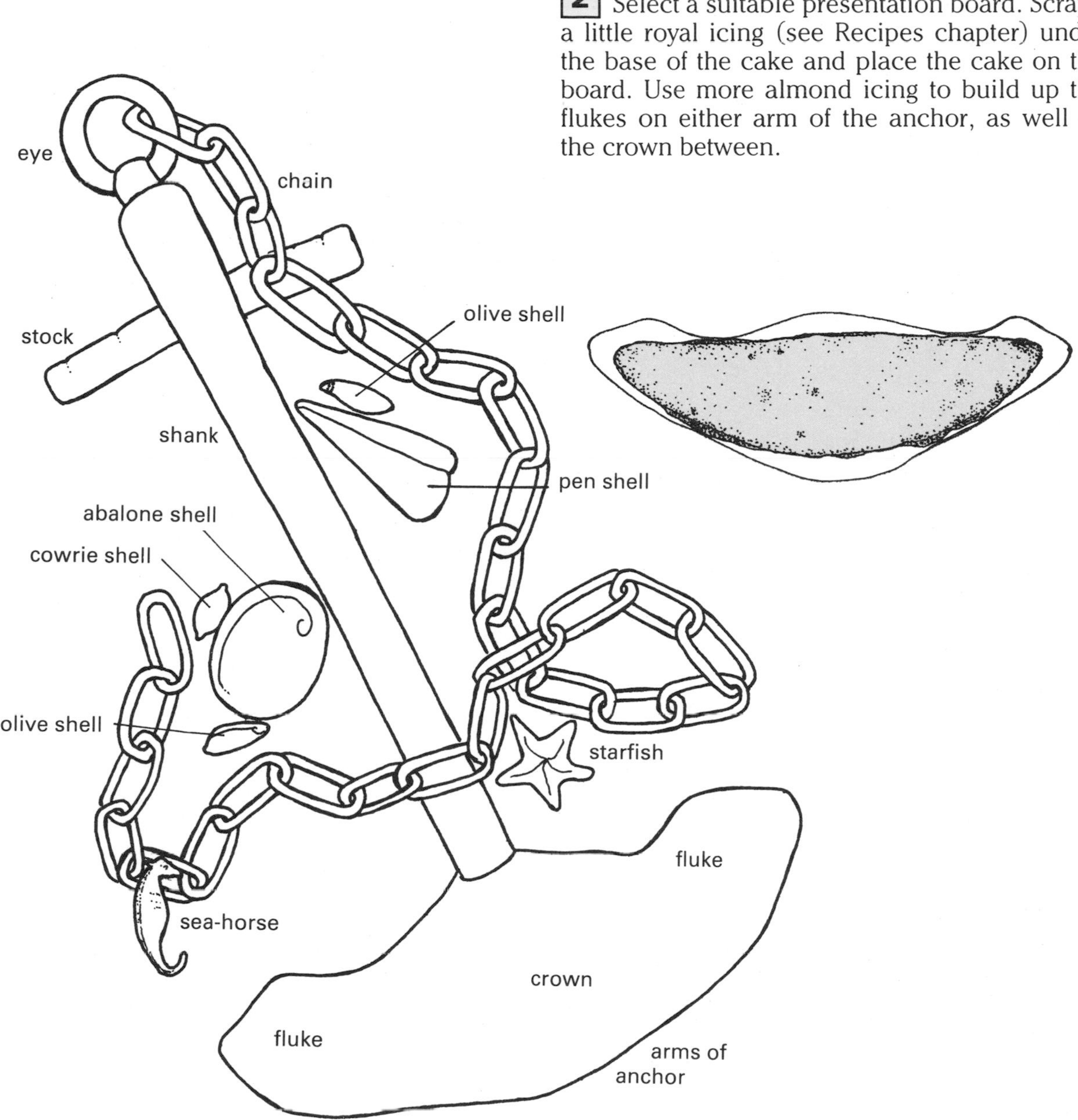

Covering the Cake

1 When the cake has cooled, release it by cutting the foil away. Fill any holes with bought almond icing.

3 Glaze the cake with some warmed apricot jam. Roll out enough almond icing or marzipan to cover the cake. Follow the instructions given in the chapter on Covering the Cake. If the cake is covered with marzipan, it should be first coloured a greyish black, because a second covering will not be necessary.

4 If you have chosen a fruit cake, you can place it aside for a few days to allow the almond icing to dry; but if your cake is a soft one, you will need to apply the second covering – of soft icing – straight away.

5 Colour soft icing a greyish black. You will need sufficient to cover the cake and form the shank. Glaze the cake with egg white, roll out the icing and cover the cake, again following the instructions given in the chapter on Covering the Cake.

Making the Parts

Shank

1 Roll some of the leftover coloured icing or marzipan into a sausage sufficiently long and fat to resemble the shank of an anchor and to look as if it could support the arms.

2 Use a thick handle to make a shallow depression in the centre of the arms where the shank goes. Moisten the depression and insert one end of the shank into it. The shank should lie at right angles to the arms. Press and push the icing of the shank wherever necessary to remove stretch marks. Smooth any cut edges that appear ragged.

Stock

Use more leftover soft icing or marzipan to form the cross-piece just below the free end of the shank. The stock consists of two short sausages, thinner than the shank and located to the left and right of it, at right angles. Moisten the two ends that join the shank before attaching them.

Eye

The eye at the free end of the shank is made from a long oval ring of coloured soft icing or marzipan. Moisten the eye where it will join the shank before attaching it.

Chain

Use the rest of the coloured soft icing or marzipan to make the chain. Roll out pieces into thin sausages and cut these into even lengths. Gently twist the lengths into rather rectangular links. Moisten and press together the ends of each, once they have been threaded through a previous link. The ends of the first link thread through the anchor's eye. Drape the chain casually over and around the anchor.

Additional Items

Sugar Sand

Follow the instructions given in the chapter on the Castle Cake for making sand. Sprinkle a liberal amount of sand all over the board. Ensure it is scattered right to the edge of the cake and between the chain links, as shown in the colour plate.

Pen Shell

The fragile-looking pen shell is found in warmer Australian waters, in the Mediterranean and along the warmer parts of the American coastline.

1 Roll out a piece of gum paste (see Recipes chapter) to a thickness of 1–2 mm. Roll out just enough paste to make one shell at a time. A suggested size for the shell is 9–10 cm in length by 3–3.5 cm in width at the widest part. The shell is made up of two long, triangular halves held together by a hinge.

2 If a real sample is available, lightly dust the underside of one of its halves with cornflour. Press the rolled-out paste against it so that the paste takes on the shape of the shell. Remove excess paste by rubbing against the edges of the shell. Smooth the paste edges by pressing them against the edges of the shell. If you do not have a real pen shell, use the number 11 cutter used for the Swans.

Repeat the process to make the other half of the shell.

3 Use the end of a cocktail stick to mark appropriate indentations in the top of the shell halves. The pen shell has a series of fine lines along its length, giving it the appearance of being divided into very small wedges. The markings can be reproduced by placing the two paste halves over the outside of the real shell, pressing down, then reshaping the paste.

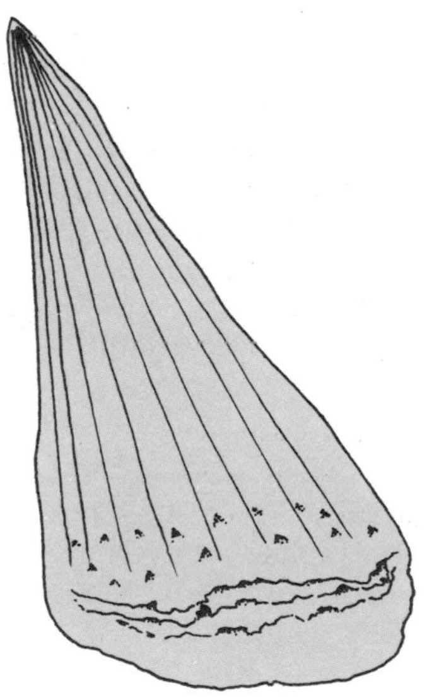

4 Set the shell halves aside to dry on a bed of cornflour.

5 Paint the lines and markings of the pen shell on the paste halves, using a very pale grey or a soft golden sand colour or a combination of the two.

6 Pipe a little royal icing at the inner points of both halves and press the two together.

7 Set the completed shell aside to dry thoroughly on a bed of cornflour.

Abalone Shell

These shells are sought, not for their outer appearance, but rather for their inner, beautiful, rich mother-of-pearl tones. The inside of the shell can sometimes be in very pale tones of pink and mauve, but more often its colours are quite bright greens, blues and pinks. Therefore, when you are making this shell, pay particular attention to the inside surface so that the rich inner colours are captured.

1 Take a piece of gum paste large enough to make one shell and roll it out to a thickness of 1–2 mm. Lightly dust the inside of an abalone shell with some cornflour. Place the rolled-out paste on the inside and press and smooth its surface so that it takes on the curve of the shell. If you do not have a shell cut the shape out with an oval cutter.

2 Remove excess paste by pressing against the edges of the shell. Smooth the paste edges out by pressing them against the edges of the shell with your fingers. Place the sugar shell, still moulded to the abalone shell, aside to dry for 30–60 minutes. Remove the paste from the shell and allow it to dry for 12 hours on a bed of cornflour before colouring it.

3 Paint the inside of the paste shell in glitter or frost tones of blue, green, pink and mauve. It is best to do this colouring with petal dust, because it gives a more natural appearance. If glitter dusts are not available, colour the inside with ordinary petal dust or pastels, then brush over the colouring with dry gold or silver powder. The underside of the shell can be painted in tones of pale grey.

Cowrie Shell

These attractive shells were once used as money in primitive societies. The cowrie shell in the colour plate is a replica of the lynx cowrie.

1 Form an olive 3 cm in length and 2 cm in diameter from a piece of gum paste. Pinch one of the ends nearly to a point. Make a flattened base for the shell, but leave the top curved.

2 Use a suitable tool, such as the blade of a pair of scissors, to make a line in the olive along its underside. Be sure to check where the division is located on the real shell. Make a series of small lines in the paste along either side of the line.

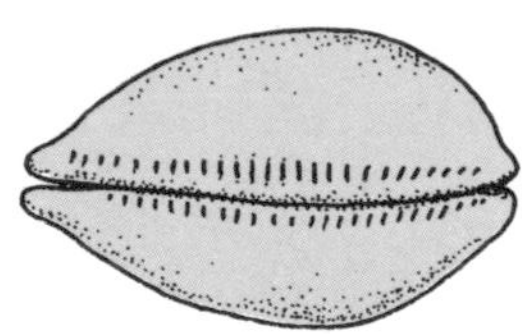

3 Set the shell aside to dry in cornflour before colouring it.

4 Colour the shell in shades of mauve and paint brown spots over the surface.

Olive Shells

1 Take a piece of paste large enough to form a small olive about 1.5 cm in diameter by 3.5 cm long.

2 Pinch along two-thirds of the length of the paste to form an edge, then curve this around the solid olive. Ensure one end of the shell has a small, shallow point. In the other end make a small opening, using a suitable tool (see Equipment chapter), and two curved lines along the curve of the shell.

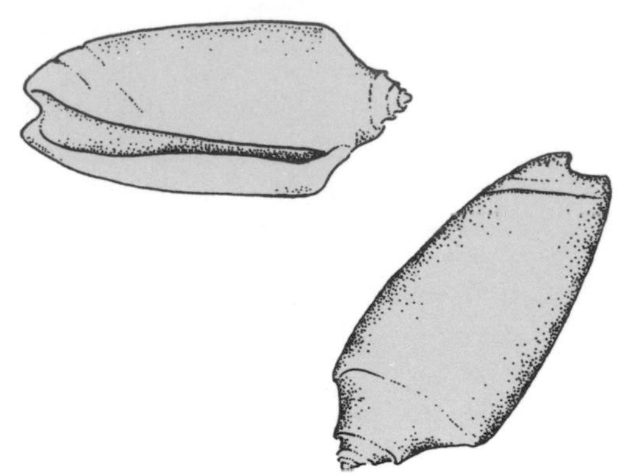

3 Place the olive in cornflour and allow it to dry thoroughly before colouring it.

4 Colour it in tones of brown, gold, mauve or ivory.

5 Make a second olive shell in the same way.

Sea-horse

1 Form a long, flat diamond, 9 cm long by 2 cm wide and 5 mm thick, from gum paste. Use a pair of scissors to trim the paste so that 4 cm at one end (the tail) is only 5 mm wide. Trim the other end also, cutting away enough paste to give the sea-horse a head and neck. Press and pull the paste so that the tail becomes smooth and rounded and is about one-third of the entire length. Press and smooth the body area, then pinch both sides of it to make it almost flat. Curve the neck and further trim the paste to form the head and snout-like mouth.

2 Use a pair of scissors to make a scale-like pattern in the tail and body, then turn the paste over and repeat the markings. Use the handle of a paintbrush to make an eye in each side of the sea-horse's head. Cut into the paste with a small pair of scissors to form the fins and feelers, but be sure not to separate them from the mass of the body.

3 Set the sea-horse aside to dry on a bed of cornflour before colouring it.

4 Colour the sea-horse a pale gold.

Starfish

1 Take a piece of gum paste and form a somewhat flattened dome about 4–5 cm in diameter. Use a pair of scissors to cut away five wedges so that the remaining paste looks like a star.

2 Press and squeeze each point of the star until it becomes longer and curves just like that of a real starfish.

3 The starfish has markings that also form a star: the lines radiate from the centre of the body to the points of the starfish. The markings can be made with the back of a blade of a pair of scissors.

4 Curve the starfish realistically, then set it aside to dry on a bed of cornflour.

5 Colour the starfish in shades of pink, mauve or pale gold.

Assemble the objects on the board as shown in the colour plate. Finish the cake by dusting it with a little skintone petal dust to create the effect of rust on the anchor.

See colour plate

on page 108

See colour plate

on page 109

Bark Huts:

L~Shaped Bark Hut Cake
Rectangular Bark Hut Cake

A cake in the form of an old bark hut can be used in many informal celebrations for adults or even children. You can get ideas for the details of old huts from drawings, photographs and cards. As well, there are many beautiful pottery replicas that can be copied. Of course, you can also go directly to the source of their inspiration. Australia's outback areas retain many ramshackle huts that can be duplicated in cake and sugar, and ghost towns offer a wealth of interesting old buildings to copy.

You can vary the size of the hut according to the number of slices you require. However, very large huts do not look as realistic as smaller ones, so an alternative method is to make two or more huts, creating a mini-town effect. In this way the cakes can not only cater for a large number of guests, they can also be used as a backdrop for other interesting features.

The colour plates show two huts of different styles and sizes. The two can form a pair, if you wish. Other features, such as outhouses, seats and a water tank, have been included and instructions for making these are given at the end of the chapter. Use the colour plates, and any of the other relevant materials mentioned, as guides for building your own interesting cakes. If a hut is to be made for children include additions such as animals or birds, using, for example, the instructions given in the Baobab Tree Cake chapter. The methods described below for making walls, roofs and other structural features can also be used for the construction of quite different kinds of buildings, such as picturesque old cottages.

A firm fruit cake is the easiest to work with, but other cakes can be used successfully. These cakes have only a three-day lifespan, so they cannot be made as far in advance as fruit cakes. If you choose a more perishable type of cake you may find it preferable to cover it with a butter icing.

Accordingly, instructions are included for covering both the L-shaped Bark Hut Cake and the Rectangular Bark Hut Cake in butter icing, as well as for covering them with soft icing. Soft icing must be used for roofs and all other firm features, so these need to be made several days before the cake is covered with butter icing.

The L-shaped Bark Hut Cake and the Rectangular Bark Hut Cake illustrated both require one quantity of cake mixture (250 g butter) and 1 kg of bought soft icing (but no almond icing) or one quantity of butter icing (see Recipes chapter). If either cake is covered with butter icing, 250 g of soft icing will be needed for the roof and other features.

L-shaped Bark Hut Cake

Shaping the Cake

1 Choose a suitable cake mixture from the Recipes chapter.

The cakes used for this work are baked in square or rectangular tins. The number '1' of the '21' novelty cake tin is also suitable. Select either a 15-cm or a 20-cm, square or rectangular tin, because the 25-cm one is too large. Remember that bark huts are usually small dwellings, so large cakes will not look authentic.

2 When the cake is cool, remove it from its tin. If the cake is square, cut away a quarter so that an L-shaped piece is left. If the cake is rectangular, remove a rectangular piece. Scrape a little royal icing (see Recipes chapter) on the base of the cake, then place the cake on a presentation board. The board should be large enough to allow for any objects or other buildings that are to be added.

Covering the Cake with Soft Icing

Before the cake is covered with soft icing it is necessary to build up any structural features and fill any holes with bought almond or soft icing.

1 If you want a pitched roof, you will need to build up icing on the top of both wings of the L-shaped cake. The built-up icing should slope down, on either long side of each wing, from a central ridge; the ridges of both wings meet at right-angles. The roof, which is made later, is draped over the built-up icing, after the icing has set. The built-up icing must be very firm to ensure that the roof is supported and does not collapse.

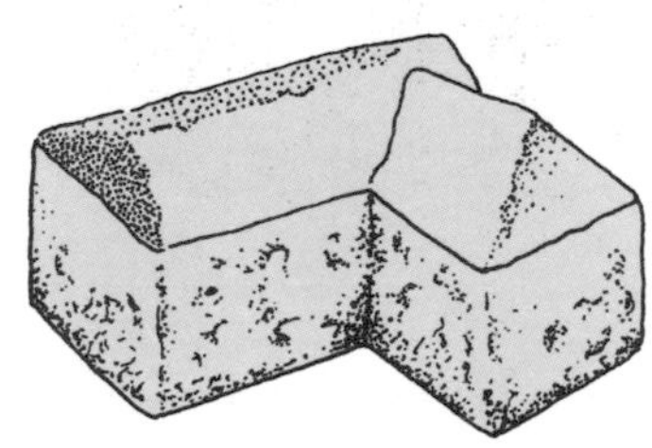

2 Colour 750 g of soft icing. The L-shaped hut illustrated was coloured a soft gold to enhance the colours painted on after the icing was dry. A mixture of ochre and brown will produce a suitable colour.

Divide the icing: 500 g is used for the hut and 250 g for the roof.

3 Glaze the whole cake with a little warmed apricot jam. Roll out a sixth of the icing reserved for the hut and cover one side with it. Cut away any excess, using a knife or scraper. Use a moulding tool (see Equipment chapter) to make indentations in the icing, creating a vertical log effect. Be sure to make notches in the 'logs'.

Repeat the process until the six sides of the cake have been covered. Continue the wall icing right up to the point of the pitched roof on the sides of the hut that end in a triangle created by the icing support for the roof. There are three such walls on an L-shaped cake. Instead of having the walls meet in a clean join at the corners, fashion the abutting edges to give the impression of logs joining.

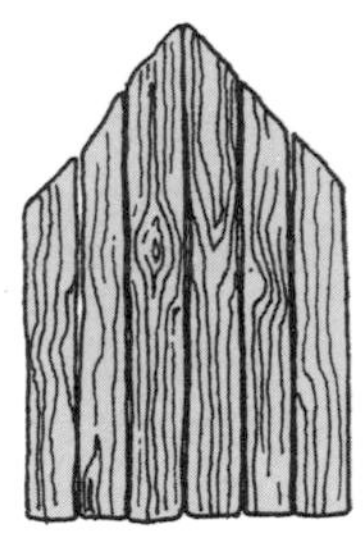

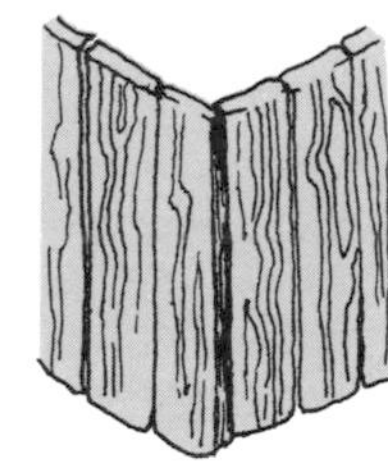

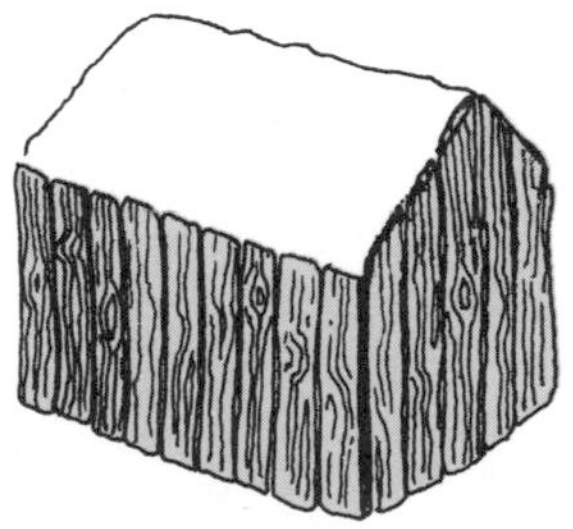

4 Use a suitable tool to make depressions in the icing for doors and windows, which are added later.

5 Roll out the icing reserved for the roof thinly and to a rectangle suitable for the roof section on the longer wing of the L-shaped hut. Use a tool with a serrated edge, such as the number 3 pottery tool, or any other suitable item, such as packing cardboard, to corrugate the icing. The grooves should run the same direction as the corrugations of a tin roof. Drape the rectangle over the built-up icing on the longer wing. Using a pair of scissors, trim off any excess length and width but allow for a verandah roof on one side and eaves at both ends.

6 Make sufficient tears and cuts in the roof to give the house a worn appearance. A series of small cuts can be made at the edges of the eaves. Use a pair of scalloped clippers or broad-ended tweezers to make crease lines along the ridge of the roof section. The edges of the roof section can also be pinched with the clippers to enhance the weathered effect. Press a depression in the roof where the other roof section is to be attached to allow for the join.

7 Roll out another piece of icing thinly to make a smaller rectangular roof section. Corrugate it as you did the first section of roof. Cut one end to an inverted V, then drape the roof section over the built-up icing of the shorter wing. The inverted V is placed so that it abuts on the other roof section. Once again trim away any excess icing, allowing for the overhang of verandah and eaves.

Use the scalloped clippers to press crease lines in the icing to suggest the ridge, and pinch the edges of the roof section in the same way as before. With the handle of a paintbrush press down along the two join lines of the roof. If any parts do not hold together, moisten them with a little water.

8 Use empty glasses or any other suitable items to support the verandah roof while the icing dries. Be sure to position the glasses in such a way that the verandah sags picturesquely. Items used as a support will have to be removed once the icing has dried; therefore it is important to arrange them so that they can be removed easily. For example, it is a good idea to place a wad of cotton wool between a glass and the icing of the verandah – the cotton wool can be removed first and the glass can then slide out freely. Cotton wool also helps the icing to retain its sags as it dries.

It is best to make house features while the icing on the cake is still soft. This will enable you to make adjustments to the hut to accommodate the features if necessary.

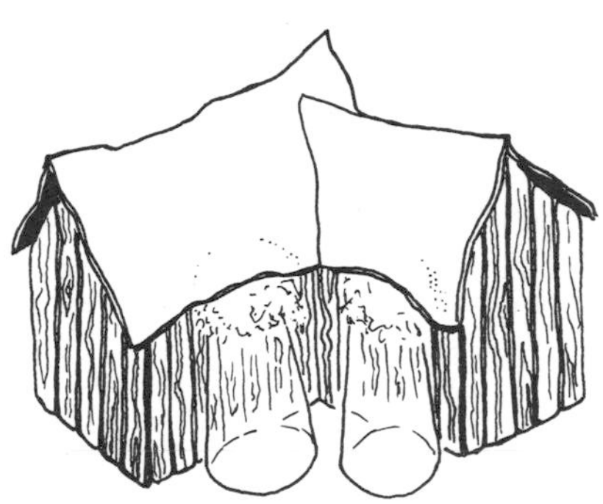

9 To form a tall chimney roll out a small piece of soft icing very thinly to a rectangle. Roll this up two or three times to form a long, cylindrical shape. Cut a diagonal section off sharply at one end, then moisten the resulting cut face with a little water. Place the chimney, slanted end down, on one side of the roof. Repeat the procedure to form another chimney for the other wing of the house. Slightly uncurl the tops of the chimneys.

10 Roll out another piece of icing thinly. Cut out several shapes for shutters and a larger piece for the door. Moisten these with water, then position them on the cake. Curve the shutters and mark a suitable log pattern on the door. The door can be left slightly open or closed. Once the features are in place, set the cake aside to dry thoroughly before doing any highlight colouring.

11 Make one or more verandah supports from icing. These can be tall, fat, straight pieces like those of the Rectangular Bark Hut Cake or, as in the case of the L-shaped Bark Hut Cake illustrated, a single Y-shaped post. To make the latter roll a piece of icing into a sausage and add a smaller piece to complete the Y. Make lines in the post with a suitable tool, then set it aside to dry in a bowl of cornflour so that the icing does not lose its shape. If greater support is required, a piece of wire may be placed in the centre of the icing while the post is being made. Add a little royal icing to both ends of the post before positioning it.

12 Give the walls and roof of the hut highlights of black, brown and ochre food colouring.

Covering the Cake with Butter Icing

1 Remember that several days before baking the cake it will be necessary to make the roof, and any other features that need to be firm, from soft icing. Such features include verandah posts, shutters, doors and water tanks.

You will need to measure the sides of the cake tin you will be using, to work out the sizes of added features. Do not forget to allow for the pitched roof sections.

2 The roof of the longer wing of the L-shaped hut is made of two sections. Roll out some soft icing into a rectangle 17 cm by 21 cm and corrugate it as described in Step 5 for Covering the Cake with Soft Icing (above). Cut the rectangle into two sections, one 17 cm by 13 cm and the other 17 cm by 8 cm. The larger one is used for the side of the roof that extends to a verandah. Place the two rectangles on a piece of waxed paper and allow them to dry for several days before using them. Note that roof sections made in this way do not have the curves of the roof of the cake covered in soft icing. However, cotton wool placed under parts of the roof as it dries will help to give it a less rigid appearance.

The roof of the smaller wing of the hut is also made of two sections. Roll out some soft icing to a rectangle 12 cm by 16 cm and corrugate it. Cut the icing into two rectangles measuring 12 cm by 8 cm. Cut away a triangular piece from the left-hand side of both to create edges that will abut on the roof of the longer wing of the hut. Set these pieces aside to dry, also.

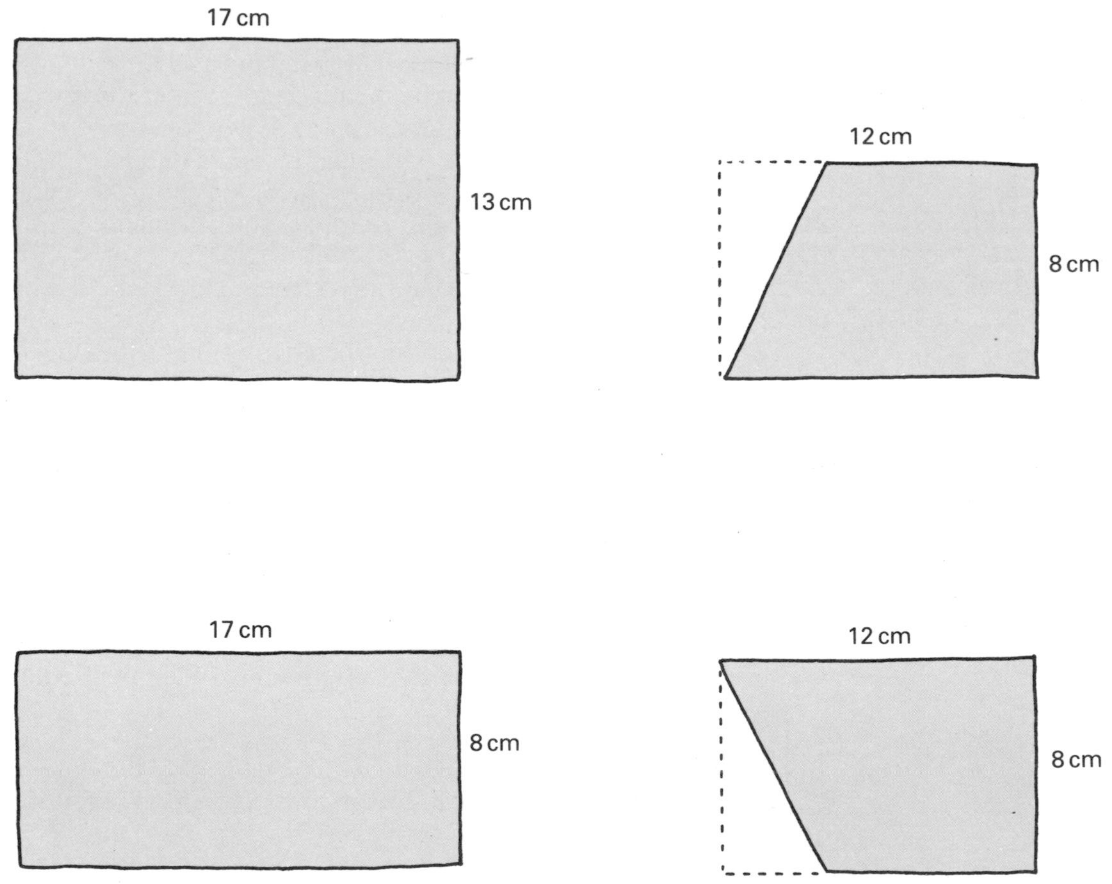

3 Make the door, shutters, chimneys and verandah posts as described in Steps 9–11 of the section Covering the Cake with Soft Icing (above). Set the items aside in a bowl of corn flour to dry.

4 Build up the top of the L-shaped cake with soft icing to form a support for the roof, following the instructions given in Step 1 of Covering the Cake with Soft Icing (above).

5 Make a quantity of butter icing (see Recipes chapter) and colour it appropriately. Spread the butter icing all over the cake's sides, including the triangular areas on the three walls that extend to the peak of the roof. Using a suitable tool, make a vertical log pattern in the icing and also make indentations for the windows and door.

6 Spread a little icing on the underside of the previously made roof sections. Position the two rectangles so that they join at the ridge of the longer wing of the hut and the larger one forms a verandah on one side.

Position the two sections that have had triangular pieces cut out of them so that they meet in a ridge over the shorter wing and abut on the roof running at right angles to them.

7 Use a little butter icing to attach the window shutters, door and chimneys to the cake.

8 Give the soft icing roof and other features black, brown and ochre highlights, using food colourings. Use paste colourings for any painting on the butter icing areas.

Sand and Logs

Once the cake has been covered with either soft or butter icing you may scatter sand made from sugar and moulded logs on the board to make the scene more authentic.

1 Make the logs in the same way that you did the verandah posts (see Step 11 of Covering the Cake with Soft Icing, above).

2 To make the sand attach a grinding blade to a food processor, then add 1 cup of sugar and ¼ of a teaspoon of ochre petal dust. Processing the sugar and colouring mixes the ochre evenly through the sugar and at the same time makes the texture of the sugar a little finer. Repeat the procedure with another cup of sugar, this time adding black petal dust. Repeat a third time, adding yellow. Sprinkle the sand over the board, allowing the three colours to merge together. Use a brush to mix the sugars further. The intermingling of the three differently coloured sugars creates a more realistic ground effect.

Rectangular Bark Hut Cake

Shaping the Cake

Bake the cake in a rectangular tin (see the notes on choosing a tin in Step 1 of the Shaping the Cake section for the L-shaped Bark Hut Cake, above).

Covering the Cake with Soft Icing

1 Remove the cooled cake from its tin and use a little soft icing to fill any holes or spaces.

2 Take 750 g of soft icing and colour it. The Rectangular Bark Hut Cake illustrated was covered in brownish black icing; added features were highlighted after the icing had dried.

3 Scrape a little royal icing (see Recipes chapter) on the base of the cake, then place the cake on a presentation board. To build up an icing support on top of the cake for the roof, follow the instructions given above in Step 1 of Covering the Cake with Soft Icing for the L-shaped Bark Hut Cake. This hut requires only a low-pitched roof since one of its main features is a large verandah.

4 Divide the remainder of the icing: two-thirds is used for the walls and one-third for the roof. Assemble the walls and roof of the hut following Steps 3–8 given above in Covering the Cake with Soft Icing for the L-shaped Bark Hut Cake (ignoring the instructions for adding a wing to a rectangular hut).

Make house features while the icing is soft so that where necessary they can be adjusted.

5 To make a stone chimney take any scraps of leftover icing and roll them into a large, fat sausage. Make it about 2 cm thick at one end and fatter at the other. The piece should be a little taller than the height of the house and roof combined. Brush a little water on one side of the sausage, then place it against an end wall of the hut so that it looks like a chimney. Adjust the roof, if necessary.

Use a suitable tool (see Equipment chapter) to mark a rough stone effect the full height of the chimney. Use a balling tool to impress a hole in the top of the chimney.

6 To make the shutters, door and verandah posts follow the instructions given above in Steps 10–11 of Covering the Cake with Soft Icing for the L-shaped Bark Hut Cake.

Covering the Cake with Butter Icing

To prepare the roof, shutters, door and verandah posts follow the instructions given above in Steps 1, 2 (paragraph 1) and 3 of Covering the Cake with Butter Icing for the L-shaped Bark Hut Cake, but make the two sections of the roof 19 cm by 13 cm and 19 cm by 9 cm; follow steps 4, 5, 6 (paragraph 1), 7 and 8 of the same for icing the cake and assembling the components.

Outhouse

Outhouses of all shapes and sizes can be found in outback Australia. Many are so worn and weary it is amazing they still stand. Use your imagination to make a particularly striking replica. The small huts shown in both the colour

Anchor and Chain Cake

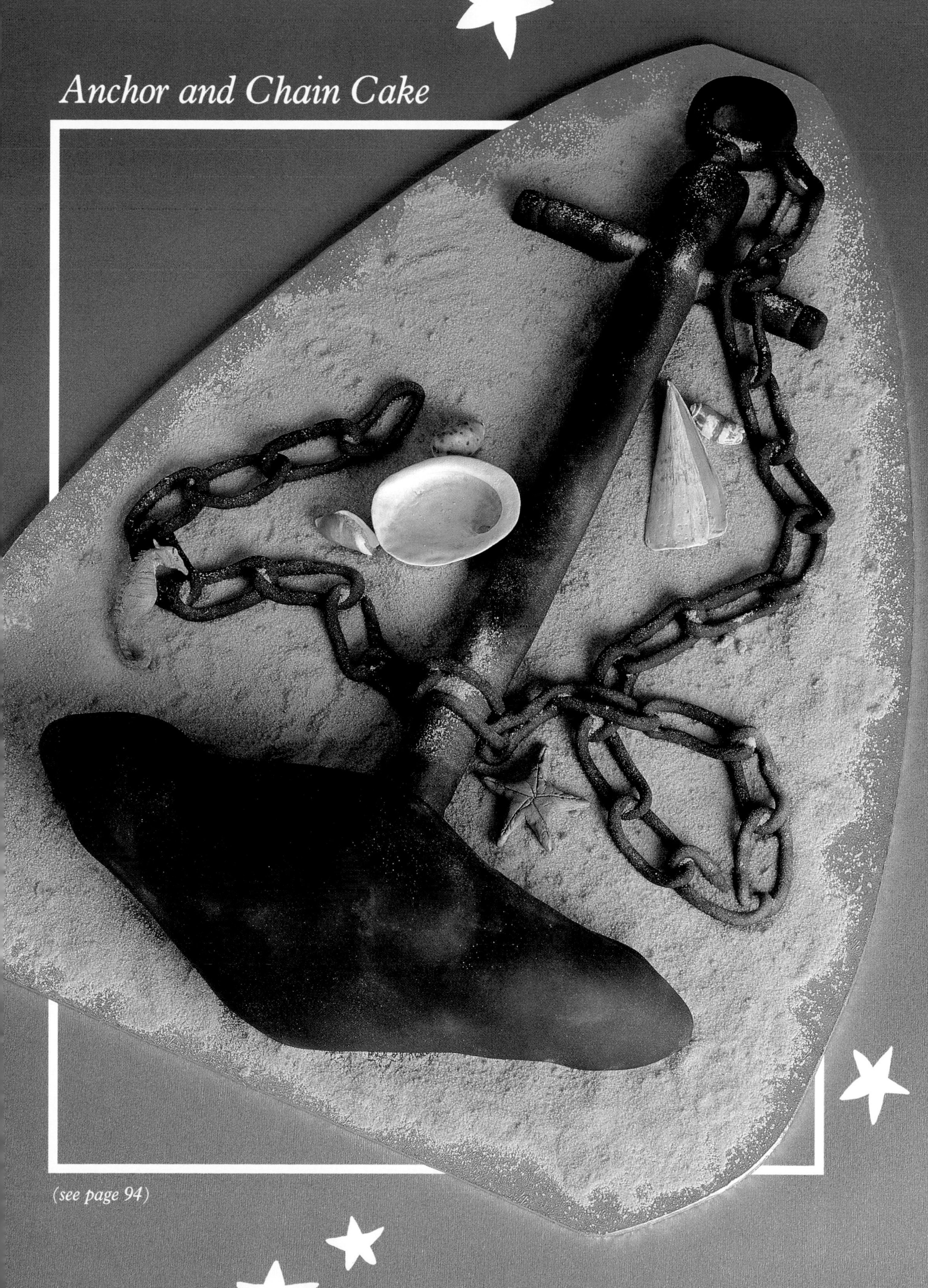

(see page 94)

L-shaped Bark Hut Cake

(see page 100)

Rectangular Bark Hut Cake

(see page 100)

Banksia Cones

(*see page 151*)

plates are examples of the outside dunnies (lavatories) so prevalent in outback Australia.

No cake is required for the building: it is made entirely from soft icing.

1 Roll out some suitably coloured soft icing. It will need to be reasonably thick so that when the sides are assembled they hold together. Cut out three sides and one door. Mark the icing to resemble logs and make chinks in the 'wood', if desired. Place the pieces on waxed paper and allow them to dry for at least three days.

2 Using some soft icing, make a small dunny can with a seat, and any other appropriate features. Set them aside to dry.

3 Place the dunny can in the centre of the spot where the outhouse is to be built. Assemble the sides of the building around it, joining them with a little royal icing. Use cotton wool inside for support, if required.

4 Make a roof for the outhouse, using the method described earlier for making soft icing roofs for bark huts covered with butter icing. If support is required to give the roof some height, place a folded paper serviette inside the building. Allow the icing to drape over the serviette, then remove the napkin when the construction is dry.

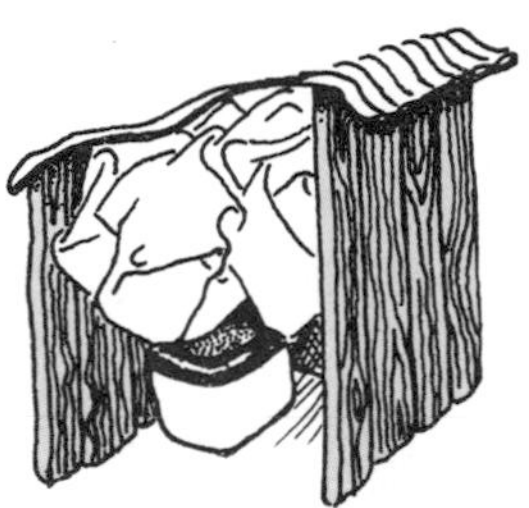

5 Place the door into position when everything else is complete.

Water Tank

Water tanks are a very important domestic feature in the outback where there is usually no running water available. You can use them to great advantage on your board, because they usually look wonderfully derelict. Worn-out water tanks are also used for storing wood.

1 Roll out a piece of soft icing to a rectangular shape and corrugate it.

2 Turn the rectangle over and place cotton wool on it. Roll it into a cylindrical shape around the cotton wool and moisten and press the ends to join them securely. Turn the tank upright and curve its top and bottom.

3 Set the tank aside to dry thoroughly in a bowl of cornflour.

4 Roll out another piece of icing and cut out a small square for the top of the water tank stand. Set this aside to dry, also.

5 Make a sausage from some soft icing and cut it into four small posts for the water tank stand. Mark them to look like wood, then set them aside to dry.

6 Place the water tank on the top piece of the stand, using a little royal icing to keep it in place. Scrape more royal icing on the tops and bases of the supports and position them somewhere beside the hut. Scrape some icing on the four underneath corners of the stand's top, then position it, with the tank, on the posts.

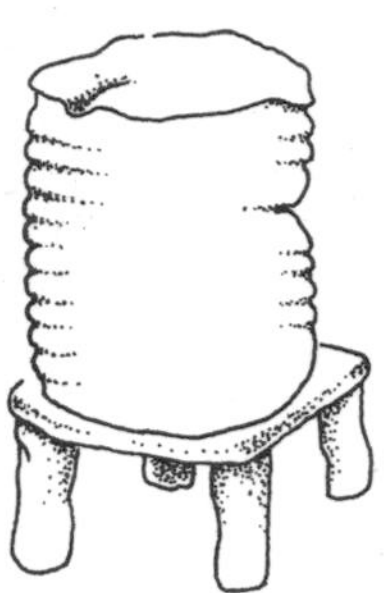

7 Make more tanks if you like and place these wherever appropriate.

Other Items

Bark huts are usually surrounded by all sorts of litter and paraphernalia: log seats, fences and, of course, small heaps of firewood. Shape sausages of soft icing into seats and logs, then mark them appropriately with a tool. When these have dried, colour and scatter them on the board.

Grass

Grass is easily made by placing different shades of green soft icing in a garlic crusher and then squeezing them. Brush either water or a little royal icing on the clumps of grass before you place them on your board.

Final Colouring

Highlight the hut and other items with brown, gold and black food colouring. Where extra details are required, add these by brushing on dry petal dust. A little methylated spirits on your brush will darken any highlights. Silver dust is ideal for the roof and water tanks. This can be used dry or moistened with water or methylated spirits. Use an appropriately coloured petal dust for rust markings on the roofs and water tanks. The chimneys can have a little soot lingering around their tops or on the surrounding tin roof. This can be gently painted or dusted on with black petal dust.

When assembling a number of huts together, make sure they are in similar shades. Do not forget to scatter some sugar sand around the buildings as a final touch (see the instructions for making sand in the section on the L-shaped Bark Hut Cake).

See colour plate

on page 128

Rustic Boots

Boots or men's shoes can be made in a variety of shapes and sizes. The cakes can easily be adapted to suit the person for whom they are made. If the person enjoys bushwalking or outdoor activities, the boots shown in the colour plate can be fashioned. Someone young might like something bright and smart, while a pair of conservative business shoes might suit an executive. Bright gumboots make appropriate cakes for young children.

The cakes can be large or small, depending on the number of people for whom you are catering. Exaggeratedly small or large cakes can lend humour to a celebration. It is also possible to make just one boot, especially if it is decorated with items, such as a mouse or some other small animal.

Before commencing work on the cakes, see if there is any suitable male footwear around the home, because the genuine article will help you to create realistic effects.

The cakes can either be baked as identical boots that are turned into left and right boot at the icing stage or extra bulges and curves can be worked into the cake mould to create a pair at the start. If you choose to make shoes it will not be necessary to give them as much height at their openings as you would boots.

Choose a cake mixture from the Recipes chapter. Be sure to select a cake that has some firmness, so that the final product will not collapse under the weight of the added icing. The boots illustrated were made from fruit cake.

Note that although fruit cakes are usually covered first with a layer of almond icing, then one of soft icing, only one complete covering of icing is used on these cakes. The layer of almond icing is usually applied to fruit cakes so that the fruit will not stain the outer covering; however, because the boots described in this chapter have a final covering of brown or black icing, staining will not be a problem. If you choose to create light-coloured shoes, it would be best for you to apply the traditional almond covering before the soft icing (see the Covering the Cake chapter).

The boots illustrated required one quantity of fruit cake mixture (250 g butter) and 1.5–2 kg of bought soft icing to cover the cakes.

Shaping the Cakes

1 Select two equal-sized, heavy-duty foil baking trays. Ones 19 cm square with a minimum height of 4 cm are very suitable. Carefully press out the folds at the top edges and any pleats at the corners. Be sure to retain the square shape of the tray.

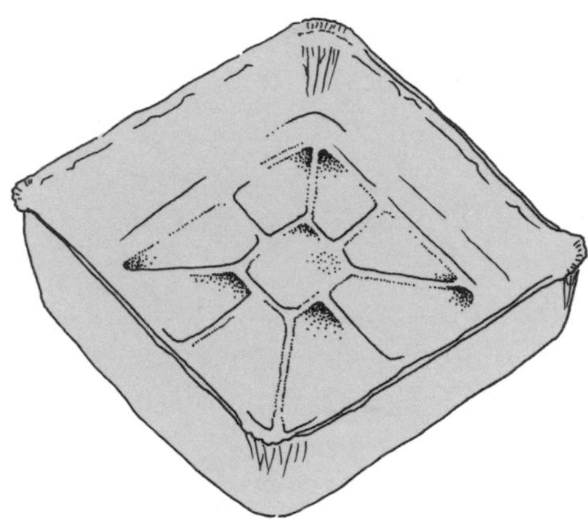

2 Cut away square pieces from two diagonally opposite corners. The sides of the squares should measure 6–7 cm.

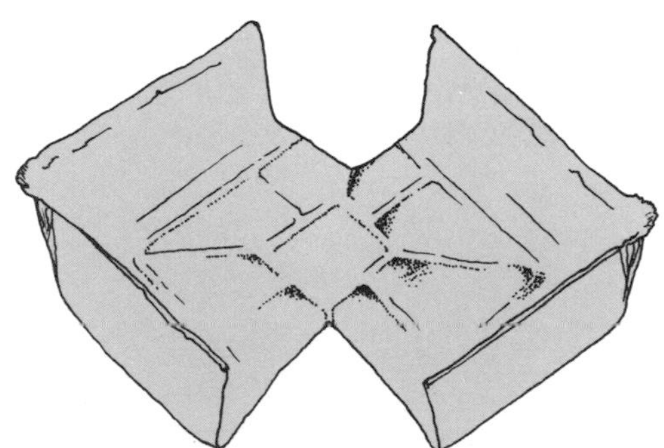

3 Repeat the process for the second tray.

4 Place the first tray in front of you with one of the two uncut corners nearest you. The corner can now be moulded into the toe of the boot. Pull up the adjacent side edges of the foil and fold the corner of the foil up and over them. Keep working these three parts of the tray until an appropriate boot shape takes form. Remember that well-worn, rustic-looking boots often have a high, rounded toe area. To form this bulge, it is necessary to make small folds and creases in the foil. Staple the joins or sew them with heavy cotton, wherever necessary. If staples are used make sure they do not dislodge during cooking.

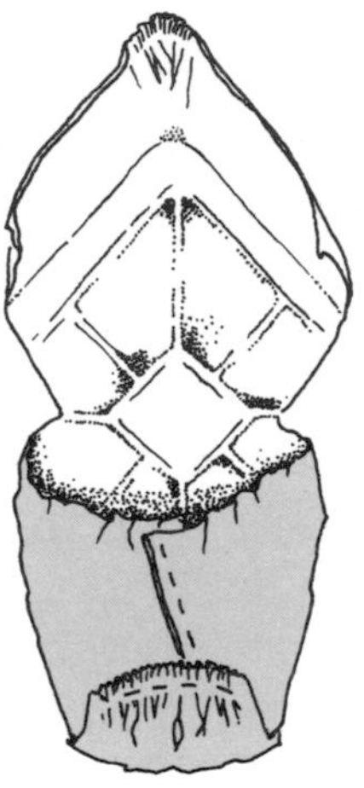

5 Repeat Step 4 for the second tray. However, ensure that you shape it into a left or right boot to make a pair with the already completed boot.

6 Turn one tray so that the remaining uncut corner is placed nearest to you, ready to be

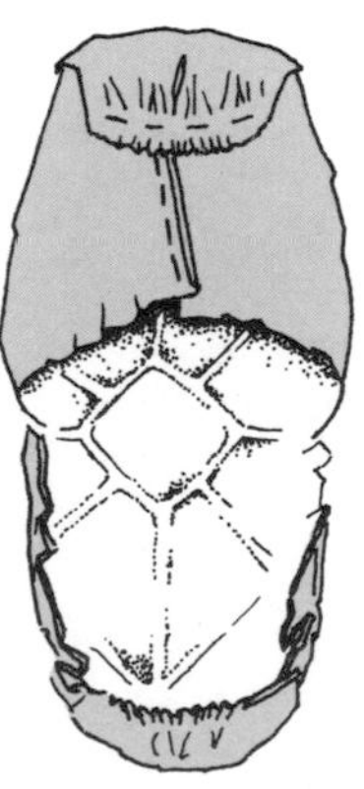

moulded into the heel of the boot. Again, pull up the edges of the adjacent sides. This time, however, draw the corner up also. It will be necessary to make large folds to ensure a good, deep heel is formed. Trim away any parts of the foil that are not required, then staple all the overlapping folds. Ensure the base of the boot is flat and that the rear of the heel is gently curved.

7 Repeat Step 6 for the second tray.

8 Next it is necessary to adjust the insteps and soles of the boots. Push down and flatten the bases of the foil moulds. Once again you may need to make folds and creases. It is also important to shape the sides of the boots, remembering to allow for the curve of a left and a right foot. Sew or staple the sides if necessary, and then place the two foil boots beside each other. Ensure that they match in size and that their soles are flat enough to hold the cake mixture during baking. If the sides are not high enough to ensure the cake mixture remains in place, it may be necessary to add some extra foil. The extra bulk of the cakes will also ensure that they are strong enough to withstand the handling they require during decorating.

9 Place the boots on a baking tray to cook, supporting them where necessary to avoid any of the mixture spilling in the oven.

10 Release the cooled, baked cakes from their foil moulds. It may be necessary to cut the foil away from the cakes so that they are not damaged.

11 If fruit cakes have been made, set them aside for a week to allow them to mature and firm up a little.

12 Fill any holes in the left-boot cake, using bought almond icing. The icing is first kneaded a little in your hands to soften it. Press small pieces into holes, then smooth the areas with a small spatula or knife. If the centre of the cake feels fragile, insert two or more bamboo skewers through it so that they run the length of the cake diagonally, crossing each other in the middle. If a piece of cake breaks off, it can be attached to the body of the cake again, using pieces of skewer. Place some icing between the broken part and the whole, then press and squeeze the two together. If any spaces remain, fill them with extra icing.

13 All boots and shoes need to have their shape further accentuated with built-up areas of icing. Place some soft icing on the toe area of the left boot: high on the right (inner) side of the boot, but sloping away a little to the left (outer) side. More icing may be required to create the folds and creases that appear in leather on the top of the toe of a boot. Shape the boot's upper so that it is wide at the front and narrower around the ankle area. The lower back of the boot also needs a build up of icing: the icing should give the illusion of a boot heel at the base and of the bulge of a foot's heel above this. Finally, build up the top of the boot to give it some height. Place a small glass or other object on the cake in the opening of the boot while the icing dries. This will ensure a hollow surrounded by icing is preserved, representing the inside of the boot where the ankle normally fits.

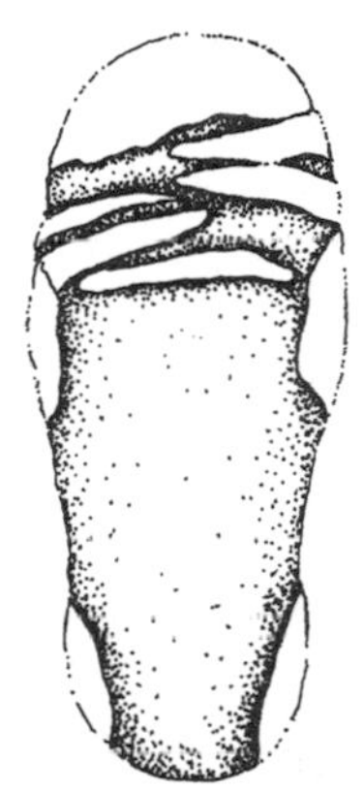

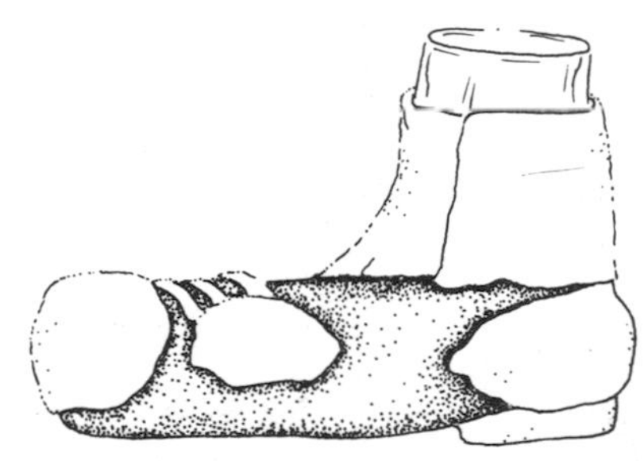

14 Shape the other boot in the same way, but remember to mould it into a right-foot boot.

15 Set both boots aside to dry for a few days before applying the complete covering.

Covering the Cakes

The boots can be fragile to move after they have been handled a lot, so it may be better to place them on a suitable presentation board before the complete covering is added.

Boots are normally either black or brown and, since dark colours can be difficult to apply uniformly at a later stage, it is best to colour the soft icing itself. Powder or paste colourings can be used.

1 Knead the powder or paste colouring into a small ball of icing until all marbling disappears. Then work the coloured ball into the rest of the icing. Repeat the colouring technique if the final colour is not strong enough. When black is required no additional colour is used. However, when brown is required you may find the addition of a little black creates a better brown for the leather.

To test the colour, form the icing into a large ball, then cut through it. If the cut faces show marbling it is necessary to knead the icing a little longer.

When the icing is ready, set it aside for an hour to allow it to firm up a little. If the icing is too soft and moist it will break and tear easily.

2 Divide the icing into two equal portions: one for each boot. Work on one boot at a time.

3 Glaze the boot with egg white. Divide the icing allotted to one boot into thirds and roll out one piece into a rectangle about 3 mm thick. Place the rolled-out rectangle over the entire front of the boot and up to the top of the laces area. The rectangle should be large enough to extend to about midway along the length of the boot. Ease the icing over the curves and creases that have been made previously. Gently press the icing so that it adheres firmly. Prick any air bubbles with a pin and ease out trapped air. Use a sharp knife to cut away excess icing from the base of the boot, then use a thin spatula to smooth down the cut edges. Use any suitable tools (see Equipment) to make creases and folds in the boot. Press firmly around the base to form the edge where the upper meets the sole.

4 Roll out the other two portions to make two equal-sized rectangles for the sides. Keep one rectangle covered while you work with the other. Each piece extends from one edge of the front opening where the eyelets go and round one side of the boot to meet the other piece at the centre rear. Cut out a rough pattern beforehand or trim the icing to fit, once it has been placed on the side of the boot. It is necessary to glaze any parts of the boot's icing where layers will overlap. It will probably also be necessary to continue to support the inner icing area with a small glass (or some cotton wool) placed inside the boot opening. Trim the top of the icing to a suitable height. Use a pair of scissors to cut away any excess at the base of the boot, then press and shape the heel of the boot.

Repeat the procedure for the second side of the boot. Press the rear seam firmly to ensure the icing merges.

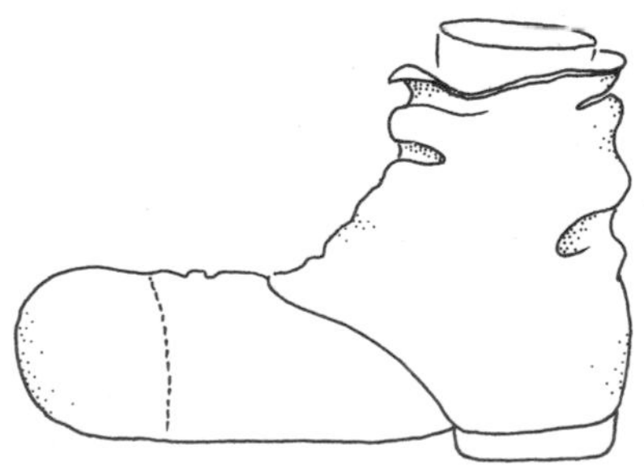

5 Roll out a small piece of icing and cut out a tongue. Moisten its base, then gently place it inside the boot so it shows between the two edges of the front opening.

6 Bend all the top parts of the icing to give the boot a well-worn look. Use a suitable tool to make a series of small, short stitch lines in the boot (use the colour plate as a guide). Make eyelets for the laces, using a skewer.

7 Roll out long, thin sausages of icing for the laces. Insert the laces, making sure you bend and twist them so that they look realistic.

8 Use a small amount of suitably coloured royal icing (see Recipes chapter) to make mud patches and apply them to the boot in appropriate places.

9 To cover the second boot, repeat Steps 3–8, but remember to allow for the differences between the right and left boots.

10 Set the boots aside for two or three days to dry well. Once they are dry, suitable final touches can be added. Brush a little petal dust in browns and ochres over parts of the boots to give them a loved and well-worn look.

See colour plate

on page 129

Girls' Shoes

You will have great fun choosing a pair of women's shoes for this cake: the range of colours, shapes and styles is endless. Choose shoes to suit the occasion being celebrated and the age and interests of the guest-of-honour. The instructions given for the cakes shown in the colour plate can be readily adapted to your needs. You can make just one shoe or a pair – or even place the shoes next to a pair of men's shoes, such as the old boots described in the chapter on the Rustic Boots. The Girls' Shoes can also be adapted for children of all ages. You may like to make them the basis for an 'Old Woman in the Shoe' cake. Although young children's shoes themselves offer inspiration for cakes, remember to make the replicas large enough to cater for a number of people.

High-heeled shoes can be made, but you may find it necessary to support the shoes with small boards, which are placed with the uppers on sugar heels. Alternatively, you can simply place high-heeled shoes on their sides.

When making shoe cakes always use either a photograph or a real pair of shoes as a guide.

The cakes shown in the colour plate include a pair of beaded socks to give them some height and further interest. Adding socks to the shoe cakes also overcomes the problem of camouflaging the inside of the shoe openings. Pantyhose or other apparel can be chosen instead of socks. Again, photographs, such as those in shoe advertisements, will give you ideas.

Select a firm cake from the Recipes chapter. If male and female shoes are to be presented side by side, it may be interesting to use different recipes for each.

Bought soft icing is used for the final covering of the cakes. The icing can be coloured any shade because ladies' footwear is available in a multitude of colours. If a very light-coloured icing is to be used, it is best to cover all the cake, regardless of whether it is a fruit cake or not, with a very thin layer of bought almond icing prior to the application of the soft icing to protect the outer covering from discolouring. If, as in the case of the shoes illustrated, the shoes are to be a bright, strong colour the almond covering will not be required because the final colour should not be affected by fruit stains. The shoes illustrated required one quantity of fruit cake mixture (250 g butter) and 250 g of soft icing for the white socks and 1.5–2 kg for the red shoes.

Shaping the Cakes

1 The pair of shoes is made from two equal-sized, heavy-duty foil baking trays. Tins 19 cm square are suitable. Press out the machine-made folds and creases so that the foil is easier to bend and shape.

Cut away 6-cm-square pieces from two diagonally opposite corners of one tray. Cut the second tray in the same way.

2 Place the first tray diagonally so that its cut edges face left and right. The corner closest to you is moulded to become the toe of the shoe.

3 Cut small nicks along the sides adjacent to the corner nearest you to make the foil easy to mould. Push these sides up a little to allow for the height of the foot and overlap them at the top of the toe. The toe formed should be fairly large and pointed. Staple or sew them together. Once the toe is stapled or sewn, mould it again to create creases and bulges that will make the shoes more realistic. Ensure that the point of the shoe is accentuated and turns up slightly.

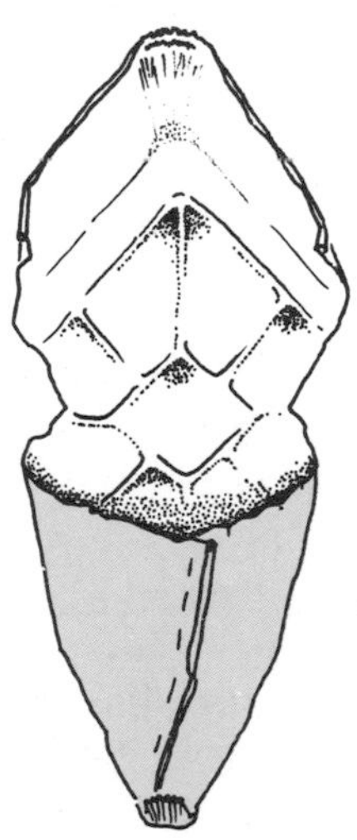

4 Turn the tray completely around so that the unworked half is in front of you.

5 Begin to form the heel of the shoe: pull up the side edges of the foil and make a series of deep folds. Women's shoes are usually quite narrow at the heel, so shape the foil accordingly. Trim away any excess foil, then staple or sew the overlapping folds.

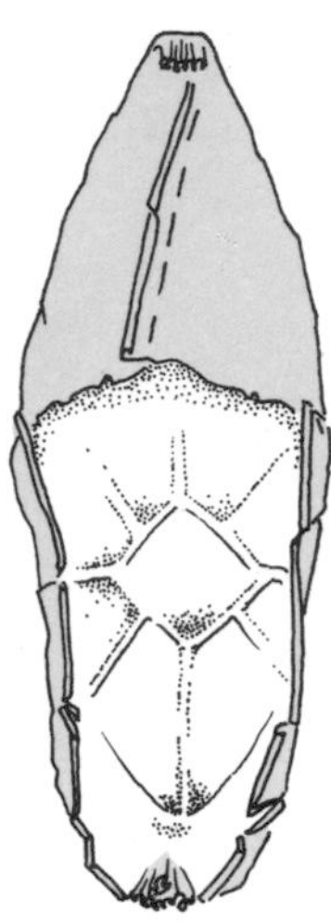

6 The instep of the shoe can now be shaped. Again, this is usually narrow. If the shoes are to be flat heeled, a small curve is pressed into the sole to suggest the arch of the instep. This is not necessary when you are making high heels. Trim and staple or sew the side folds together, making sure you allow enough height to give the shoes a realistic appearance – if there is not enough foil at the sides, staple on some extra pieces, then trim them.

7 Make the second shoe in the same way as the first, remembering that it has to be one of a matching pair.

8 Place the two cake moulds on a baking tray during cooking to catch any drips that occur.

9 It is best to rest fruit cakes for a week or two after they have been baked to allow them to firm up a little. Cakes other than fruit cakes are ready to shape and cover once they have cooled.

Release the cakes from the foil trays by cutting open the moulds. Gently ease the cakes away from the foil, being careful not to accidently break off small sections from vulnerable areas.

10 Use some almond icing to fill any holes or spaces. For best results knead it in your hands until it is warm and soft, then push pieces into the holes. Use a small spatula or knife to press and flatten the icing. Fill in any spaces by using the build-up technique. Press and mould the icing to fit the general shoe shape.

If the cake is soft and fragile, particularly at the narrow instep, insert two or three bamboo skewers along its length to reinforce it. No small board supports are required for the shoes in the colour plate, since they do not have high heels. However, if you are making high heels, add these small supports at this point.

11 Any particular areas that require a build up of icing should be dealt with now. Build a small heel, an instep and a toe for each shoe. Make sure that the heels do not become too large. Slightly hollow the openings for the feet in the shoes. Do not forget to shape a left and a right shoe.

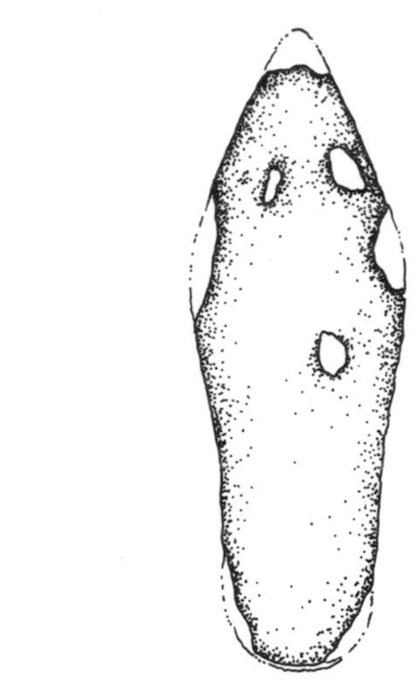

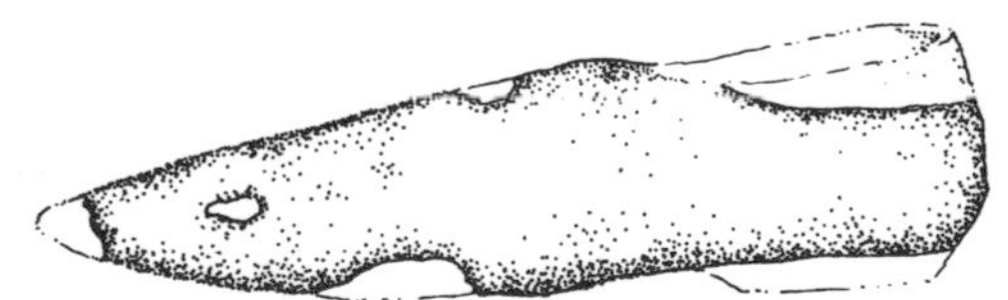

12 Set the shoes aside to dry for several days before covering.

Covering the Cakes

1 If the cakes are fragile, it is best to apply the covering after the cakes have been positioned on a presentation board, to avoid unnecessary moving.

Add a covering of bought almond icing, if the colour of the shoes is to be pale. The almond icing is placed on the cake in the same way as the soft icing (see Steps 4–5 below).

2 Knead one sachet of red food colouring into a small ball of soft icing. Knead the ball well until the colour is evenly distributed. If the icing becomes too soft and paste-like, add some cornflour or even a little more soft icing to help keep it firm. Knead the red ball into the larger mass of icing reserved for the shoes until the colour appears to be even. To test, roll the icing into a ball and then cut through it. If marbling shows, the icing will need to be worked again. Repeat the kneading and cutting until an evenly distributed colour is achieved.

3 Cover the icing and set it aside to rest for several hours before using. Note that if the icing is used while it is too soft and moist it will tear and be difficult to handle.

4 Halve the icing. Cover one half and set it aside while you work on the first shoe.

Roll out the icing to a large rectangle 3 mm thick. Measure the cake and ensure that the rectangle is both long and wide enough to completely cover it. Glaze the cake with egg white. Turn the board so that the length of the shoe is facing you. Pick up the icing on the rolling pin and gently place it over the cake (see Covering the Cake chapter). Ensure that the entire cake surface is covered. If it is not, remove the icing, knead and roll it again, then reapply it.

Allow the icing to gently ease over all the surfaces of the shoe. Press firmly against the top and sides. Smooth down the base edges of the icing and ensure that there are no air locks between the icing and the base of the cake. Prick any air bubbles with a pin. Trim away excess icing at the base of the cake.

5 Use a small spatula and any other suitable tools (see Equipment chapter) to press features into the shoes. Shape the icing at the base of the shoe into sides of a sole. Pull the icing together at the front base where the point upturns. It may be desirable to use a pair of scissors to cut away excess icing, because this ensures that the cut edges can join neatly. Squeeze and press the icing to remove any join lines. Form a shallow depression at the opening for the foot.

6 Use a cocktail stick to indent stitch lines in the icing at the front and back of the shoe.

7 Take a bundle of large, white stamens and cut off the excess cotton lengths. Use a small blossom cutter to make a flower pattern around the toe of the shoe. Place a stamen in the centre of each flower imprint.

8 Roll out some of the icing off-cuts into a long, 2–3-cm-wide strip. Shape this into a suitably sized bow. Small balls of cotton wool can be placed between the folds of the bow to give it a fuller look. Use another strip of icing to form the small centre band of the bow. Brush a little egg white on its underside, then place the bow at the centre top of the shoe. Insert several white stamens in the bow to look like a scattering of beads.

9 Cover and decorate the second shoe in the same way as the first, allowing, of course, for the differences between the left and right feet.

Beaded Socks

White socks with red stamens, suggesting beading, have been added to the shoes illustrated. The socks contrast well with the red shoes and provide an illusion of depth.

1 Roll out the small quantity of white soft icing reserved for the socks to a thin rectangle measuring 15 cm by 10 cm. Place some cotton wool along one of the short sides of the icing. Starting at the other short end, roll the icing into a hollow cylinder, with the rolled end overlapping the first end. Use a tool to press along the inside of the overlapping area. Ensure that the two layers of overlapping icing adhere to each other, then trim away any excess at the seam, using a pair of scissors.

Make a second small, hollow cylinder filled with cotton wool in the same way, for the second sock.

2 Glaze one shoe opening with a little egg white. Be sure to restrict this glaze to the depressed area. Lift one sock with the handle of a wooden spoon and place one of its ends on the shoe opening. Press and ease the sock into an appropriate position, making sure the join is not visible. Some of the cotton wool may need to be kept in to ensure the icing retains its hollow appearance as it dries.

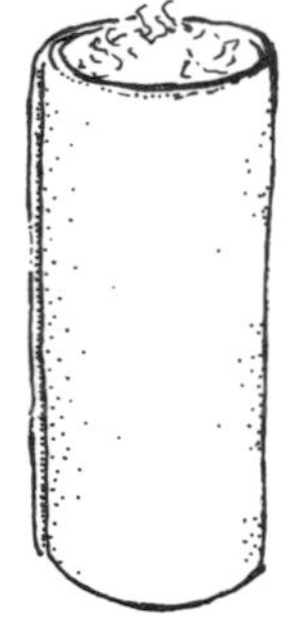

3 Cut the excess cotton lengths from a bundle of large, red stamens and insert the stamens in the top of the sock to give the impression of a band of beading. When the sock is dry, remove the cotton wool support.

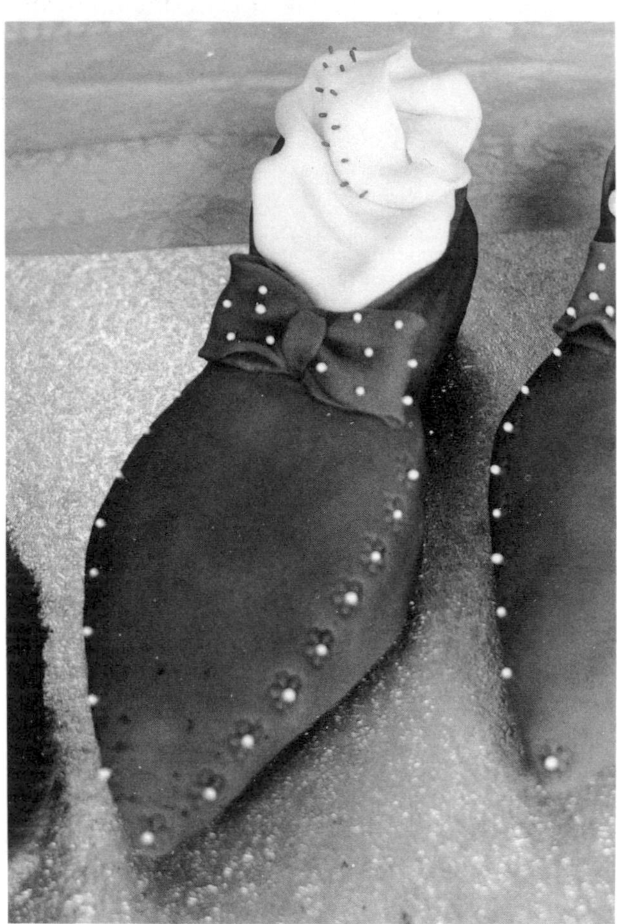

4 Repeat Steps 2–3 for the second sock.

See colour plate

on page 127

Ayers Rock Cake

The grandeur and mystery of Ayers Rock, or Uluru, makes it a rather unusual but effective subject for a cake. Present it to the traveller or nature lover or as a very different birthday cake.

The cake can be made as small or as large as you desire. The Ayers Rock Cake shown in the colour plate was cut from a cake measuring 33 cm by 30 cm. However, the heavy build up of icing required when shaping the cake takes place means that a fruit cake (see Recipes chapter) is the only suitable recipe to use.

The cake illustrated required two to three quantities of fruit cake mixture (500–625 g butter), and 3 kg of bought soft icing for the covering and a little more for the additional touches.

Shaping the Cake

The capacity of your largest cake tin may determine the size of your cake; you may also discover that the size of your oven is a limiting factor, because some of the very large tins will not fit into many of the modern ovens. However, if you wish to make the Rock very large, several square or rectangular cakes may be combined: use bamboo skewers inserted in their sides to help hold the cooled cakes in position.

1 Once you have decided on the size of your cake, use the template provided on the next double page. Enlarge or reduce the drawing on a photocopier to get your required scale.

Pattern for Ayers Rock Cake

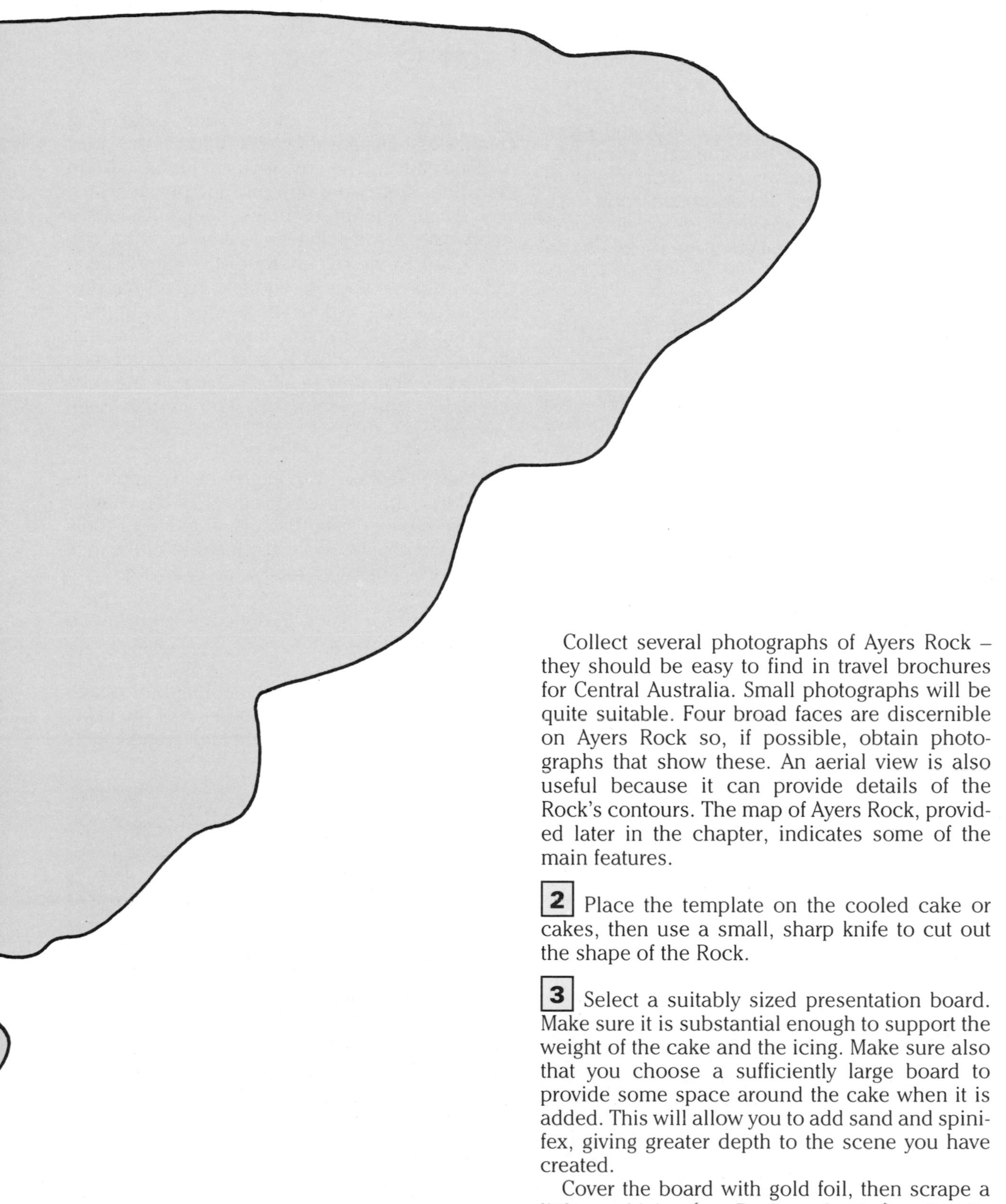

Collect several photographs of Ayers Rock – they should be easy to find in travel brochures for Central Australia. Small photographs will be quite suitable. Four broad faces are discernible on Ayers Rock so, if possible, obtain photographs that show these. An aerial view is also useful because it can provide details of the Rock's contours. The map of Ayers Rock, provided later in the chapter, indicates some of the main features.

2 Place the template on the cooled cake or cakes, then use a small, sharp knife to cut out the shape of the Rock.

3 Select a suitably sized presentation board. Make sure it is substantial enough to support the weight of the cake and the icing. Make sure also that you choose a sufficiently large board to provide some space around the cake when it is added. This will allow you to add sand and spinifex, giving greater depth to the scene you have created.

Cover the board with gold foil, then scrape a little royal icing (see Recipes chapter) on it at its centre, and place the cake in position.

4 The various details around the sides of the Rock are built up on the cake in bought almond icing. Refer to your photographs to help you model the Rock. Some of the faces of your cake will be sloped, while others will have depressions representing The Brain and various caves. Some parts will be very undulating and these may need substantial building and moulding. Knead some almond icing in your hands to soften it before using it. Use pottery tools (see Equipment chapter), skewers and a clean comb to sculpt the characteristics of the rock faces in the built-up icing.

5 Using aerial views as a reference, start to build up the contours of the Rock's top. If your cake is large, large pieces of icing will be required for this work. Smooth and press the icing into position until your cake top appears to have the waving, contoured lines that have been weathered in the Rock. Broadly, the lines slope north and south to the edges of the top from a central spine.

6 Once the shaping has been completed, cover any remaining exposed sections of the cake. Brush these areas with a little warmed apricot jam, then press and smooth almond icing over them until the cake is covered.

7 Set the cake aside for a week or two until it has become firm.

Covering the Cake

1 Colour the soft icing, using petal dust colourings because they will achieve the most realistic effects. The colours used for the cake in the colour plate were skintone and peach, with a very small amount of black added. Colour a small ball of the icing first, then add the coloured ball to the remainder of the icing. Knead well. If more colour is required, repeat the process of adding colour to a small ball, then kneading the ball into the larger mass. Note that the colour of the icing is a fraction lighter than the shade ultimately required, because the cake receives a final touch up after it has been covered.

2 Glaze the cake with egg white. To apply the icing follow the instructions given in the chapter on Covering the Cake. Be sure to use your tools and skewers to delineate any features of the rock faces that become hidden by the covering.

3 Set the cake aside to dry completely before adding highlights.

4 Brush a combination of skintone, peach and black petal dust on the surface of the cake. To reproduce the striking light and shade effects

Ayers Rock Cake

(see page 123)

Rustic Boots

(see page 113)

Girls' Shoes

(see page 118)

Cuddling Couch Cake

(see page 132)

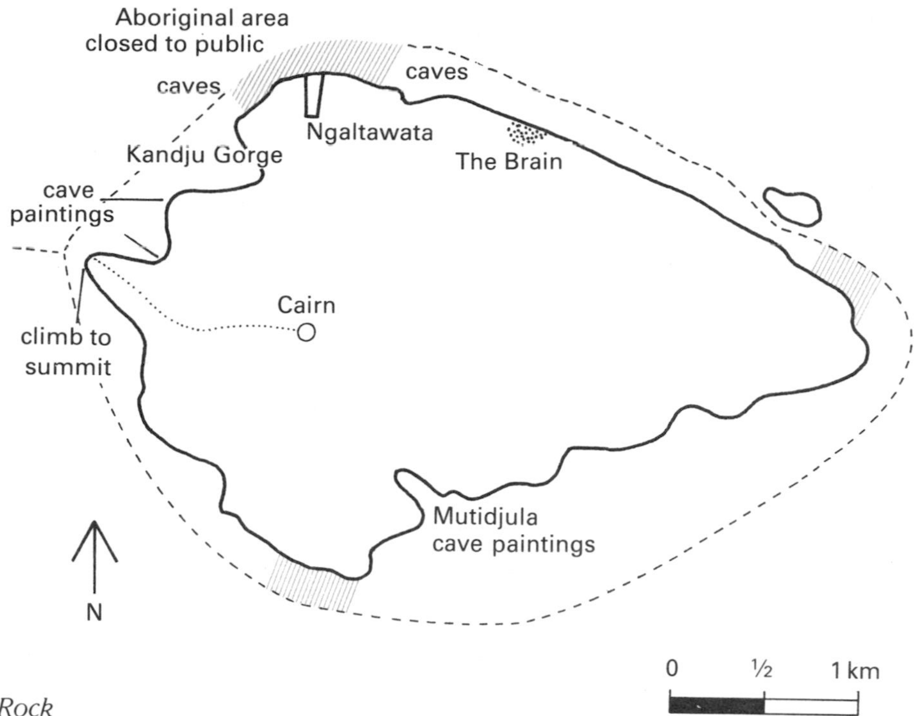

Map of Ayers Rock

of Ayers Rock the cave areas and depressions may need to be painted a little darker than the main areas, and parts of the top may need to be coloured in rich rust tones.

Final additions

Sand

1 Follow the instructions given in the Castle Cake chapter for making sand, using orange colouring.

2 Sprinkle the sugar sand around the board so that the cake begins to look like the Rock rising above the red sand of the desert.

3 Further enhance the realistic effect by sprinkling skintone petal dust on the sand adjacent to the Rock to suggest shadows.

Spinifex

1 Follow the instructions given in the Castle Cake chapter for making grass, using pale blue-green icing.

2 Scatter small clumps of grass in the sand around the cake.

3 Insert green-coloured, curved stamen cottons in the grass patches to help achieve the tall, spiky appearance of spinifex.

See colour plate

on page 130

Cuddling Couch Cake

The Cuddling Couch Cake is a wonderfully versatile cake. It can be adapted to many occasions, such as wedding anniversaries, engagements or the celebration of a new-born child. The seated people can be an elderly couple, young lovers or a family group.

The style and number of the pieces of furniture can be altered according to your tastes and the size of the party. The Cuddling Couch Cake requires a little more preparation time than some of the other fantasy cakes in the book and lots of imagination, but it is well worth making. A fruit cake mixture makes the best basis for the work (see Recipes chapter). A covering of almond icing is not required because the dark-coloured soft icing will not show any fruit stains that occur.

The cake illustrated required one quantity of cake mixture (250 g butter), and 1 kg of bought soft icing for the couch and 1.2 kg for the other components.

Shaping the Cake

For best results, bake the cake in a rectangular tin. A 20-cm tin provides the best shape; however, other sizes can easily be adapted. Note that although there is some wastage of cake, you can use the cut-out pieces for extra furniture.

1 After the tin has been filled with cake mixture, a square or rectangular ramekin dish is placed inside it. Oil the outside surfaces of the dish so that it can be removed easily when the cake is ready. Place the ramekin upside down at the centre of one of the long sides of the cake tin and against the side. Press down hard until the surrounding mixture rises to level with the ramekin's top. As the cake bakes, a depression will be formed, reducing the amount that you have to cut away.

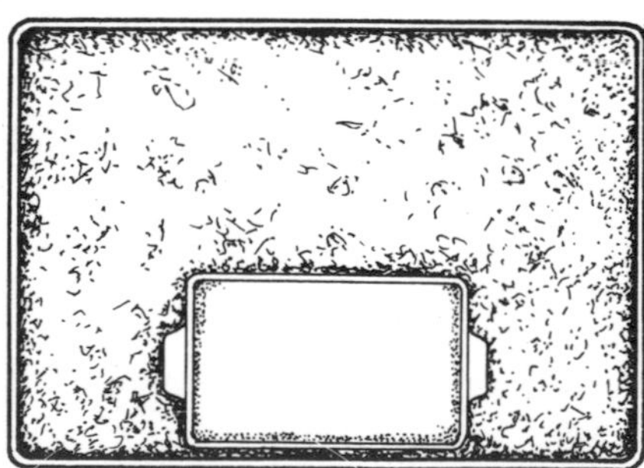

2 Remove the ramekin once the cake is cool and cut the cake to the required shape. Use some of the off-cuts to build up other areas, such as the back and arms of the couch. To do this, glaze the relevant sections of the couch with a little warmed apricot jam, then insert one or more pieces of bamboo skewer in each. The skewers must protrude a little above the cake. Place the cake pieces on them, then push the off-cuts down until they join the couch. Fill any remaining spaces with a little bought almond icing.

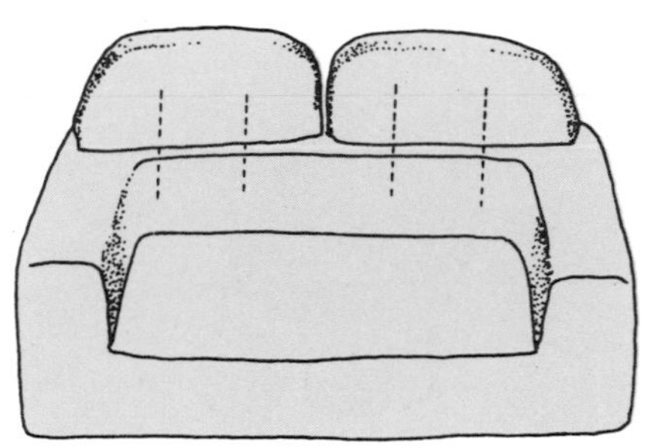

3 Build up any other sections that need more definition, with pieces of almond icing. Trim any uneven parts.

4 Set the cake aside to firm for a few days.

Covering the Cake

1 If the couch is to be coloured a dark shade, it will be best to use a sachet of powdered colouring. Work the powder into a small ball of icing, then knead the ball into the larger mass. To test the colour, roll the icing into a ball and cut through it. If the cut surface reveals no marbling, the icing is ready; if it does, knead the icing further and test again.

2 Scrape a little royal icing (see Recipes chapter) on the base of the cake, then place it on a presentation board.

3 Roll out the soft icing thinly to a rectangular shape. Glaze the cake with a little warmed apricot jam. Turn the board so that the back of the couch faces you, then cover the cake with the icing.

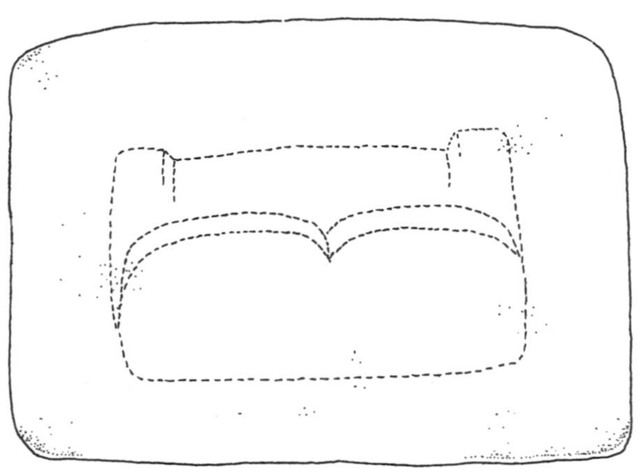

Gently press the icing down the back and along the arms of the couch. Ease the icing over the seat area, being careful not to tear it. If this is difficult to do, prick the icing in a few places with a pin so that trapped air can escape. When the icing is firmly adhering to the cake surfaces, trim off any excess, using a sharp knife or scraper. Rub gently over the covered couch until the surfaces become smooth. Use scrapers wherever necessary to get as smooth and even a finish as possible.

4 Use the leftover pieces of soft icing to make the seat cushions of the couch. Roll the pieces into a fat sausage. Flatten the sausage with a small rolling-pin into a piece resembling a mattress no longer or wider than the seat area.

Cut the flattened icing in half. Shape the halves into cushions with soft and rounded edges. Place two cushions on the couch, then give them sags and dips, using your fingers, to make them look well worn. If you would like to suggest stitching, make indentations in the edges with the tip of a fine skewer.

5 Set the couch aside to dry for a few days. In the meantime other items can be made.

Floor Rug

The rug shown in the colour plate was made from a piece of pale yellow soft icing. The design on it was created with small pieces of red, green and brown icing, but, of course, you can make your own design or use different colours, if you wish.

1 Roll out thinly yellow soft icing into a rectangle the length of the couch.

2 Dot the rug with circles of brown and green icing in diagonal rows. The diagonal lines of the carpet design (or curved lines, if you prefer) are made from very small sausages of brown and red icing, which are then interspersed with the circles. Roll across the top of the rug with a rolling-pin. The colours of the small circles and sausages will merge into the yellow of the larger piece. When the rug is flat and smooth, trim it to the required size.

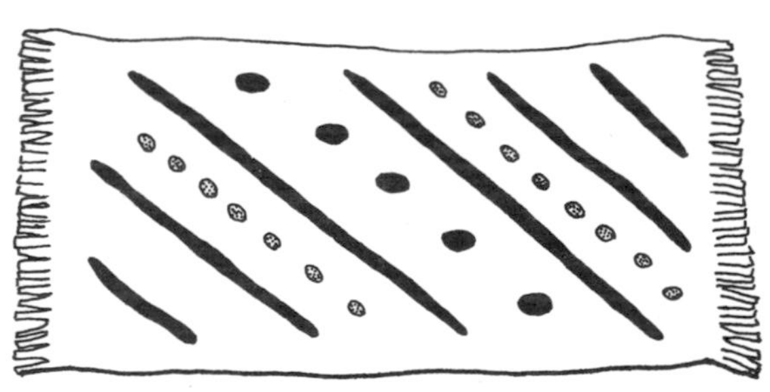

3 Use a small pair of scissors to make a series of small incisions along the two ends of the rug to create fringes. The cuts should be 2 cm long and 2–3 mm wide. Ruffle some of the small strips of the fringes. Place the rug in front of the couch and allow it also to dry for a few days.

Sugar People

The figures can be made with or without armatures to support their upper parts. If support is needed, the cotton-covered wire usually used for flower making is strong enough. Alternatively, small pieces of bamboo skewer can be placed within certain sections, so that heavier parts do not fall off.

Young Woman

1 Colour some pieces of soft icing. The young woman in the illustrated Cuddling Couch Cake requires green-coloured icing for her dress, gold for her hair, black for her shoes and skintone for her face and body.

2 Shape a piece of icing into a head and neck and insert a skewer as a support. Gently press facial features into the icing.

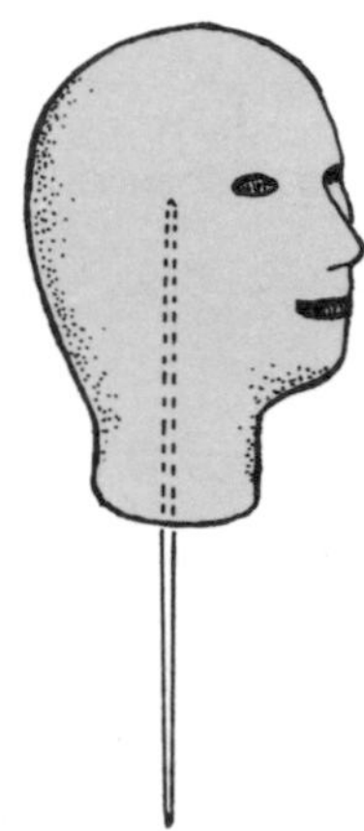

3 Form the chest and body from another piece. If you decide to insert wire as a body support, include the arms also at this stage.

Do not forget to give the young woman a nicely shaped bosom.

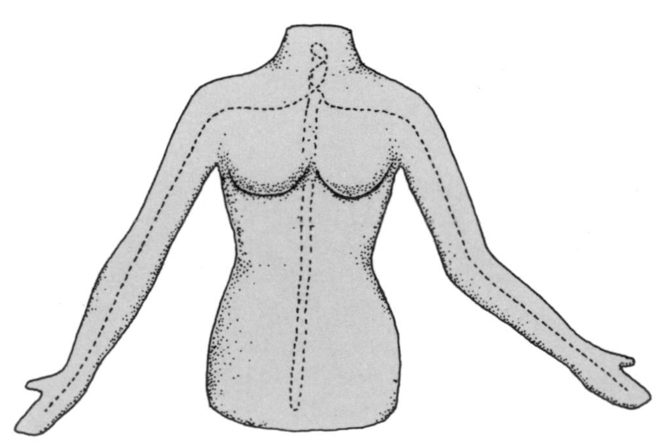

4 Make two legs, being sure to include wire supports inside them. Have the wire ends protruding a little from the legs at the top, so that they can be inserted into the icing of the body.

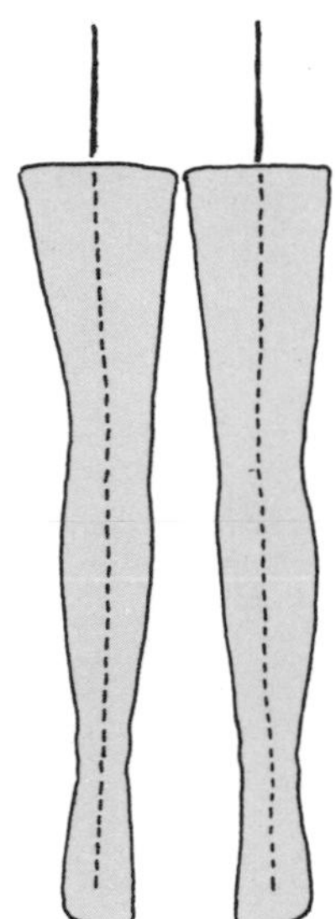

5 Assemble the figure, give it a seated posture, then place it on the couch in such a way that the icing will not become distorted or fall apart. The wires and skewer will allow some bending and adjustments to be made.

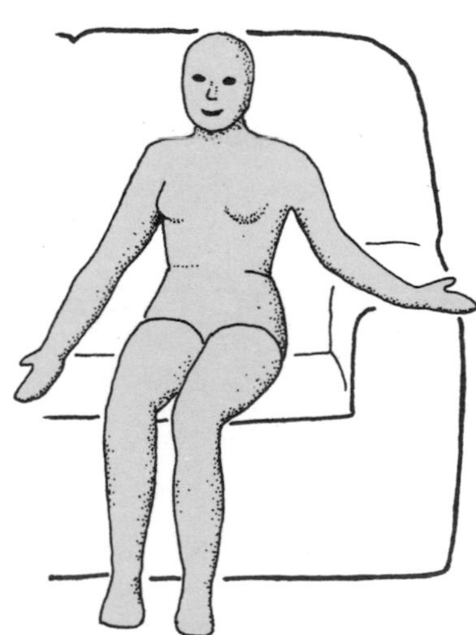

6 Roll out a piece of green icing and make garment pieces, using the patterns provided. Moisten the bodice and attach it to the body. Arrange the skirt so that it meets at the waist of the bodice. Moisten the top of the sleeves and attach them to the shoulders of the bodice. Finally, place some small pieces of white icing on the bodice to represent a collar and buttons.

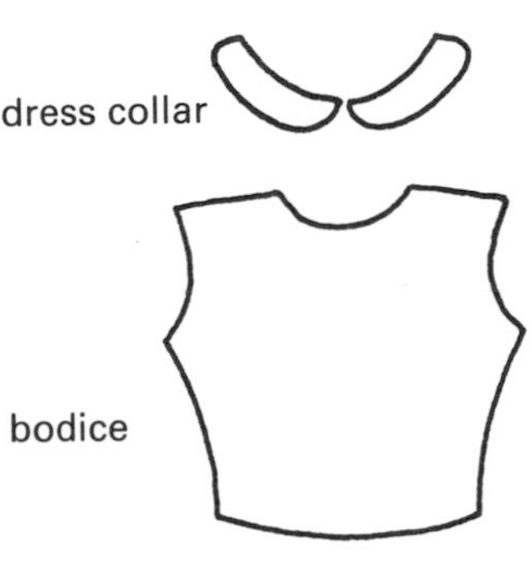

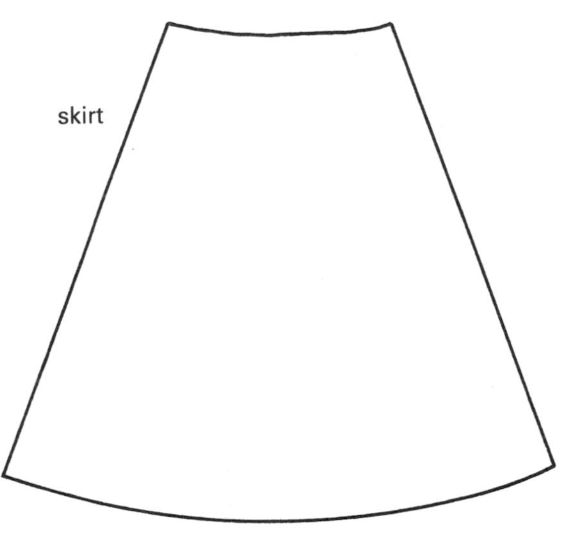

7 Press some gold-coloured soft icing through a garlic crusher to create strands of hair. Use water and a paintbrush to place them on the head. The young woman in the colour plate has been given a 1960s bouffant hairstyle.

8 Cut out two small, black pieces of icing for shoes and place them on the feet.

Young Man

1 Colour some pieces of soft icing black, white, brown, fleshtone and red, if you are copying the young man in the colour plate. Make up the head, body and legs in the same way that you did those of the young woman (see Steps 2–4 above), although obviously these will be larger and a bosom will not be required.

2 Cut out a pair of trousers from black icing, using the pattern provided.

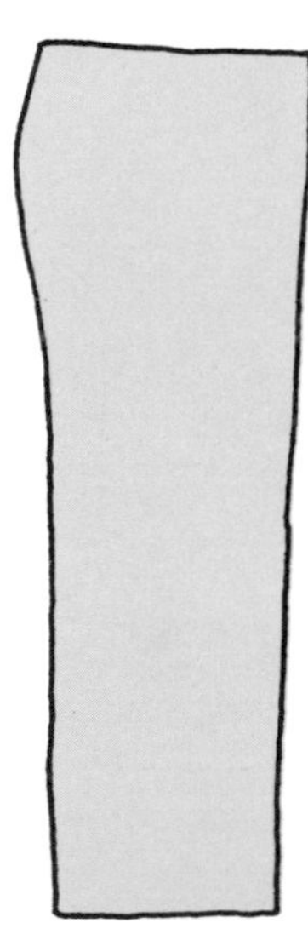

trouser leg

3 Assemble the figure, also attaching the trousers, before placing it on the couch.

4 Place a small piece of white icing down the front of the figure to represent a shirt. Use a small piece of black icing for a tie.

5 Roll out some brown icing and, using the pattern provided, cut out a jacket. Attach the jacket to the body, giving it some folds and creases. Cut out a small, white collar and attach it to the shirt.

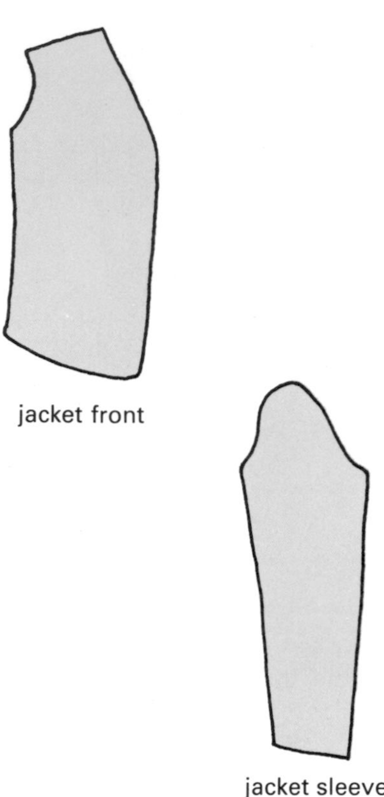

jacket front

jacket sleeve

6 Use black icing for shoes and some more, pressed through a garlic crusher, for strands of hair. Attach the hair, using water and a paintbrush.

7 Make a small, red parcel, tied with a white strip of icing, and place it in the young man's hands.

Decorations

Cat

1 Take a piece of beige-coloured soft icing and shape it into a long, fat tear-drop. Squeeze the top part between your thumb and index finger to form a head. Pull some of the icing at the other end into a tail. Pinch out four short legs.

2 Mould suitable features on the head, including ears. Curl the body, then place the cat beside or on the rug.

Coffee Table

1 Roll out some brown icing and cut out a triangle for the top of the coffee table. Roll out some more to a thin sausage. Cut the sausage into three legs, then set all the parts of the table aside to dry.

2 Assemble the table, using some royal icing to join the parts.

Tea-set

1 Take a small quantity of gum paste (see Recipes chapter) and colour it – the set in the illustration is cream. Add a little soft icing to make the gum paste more malleable, if it feels too firm.

2 Roll out four very small, pea-shaped pieces of paste to form two saucers and two cups. Press two of the pieces into small, flat circles and place them on a piece of foam. Press down on the centres of the saucers to give them a curved shape.

3 Hollow and shape the remaining two balls on the rounded end of a curler pin to form cups. Ensure both cups are the same size. Set them on the saucers and place them onto the assembled table.

4 Form a ball for a teapot and two smaller balls for two other plates from some more paste.

Make the two plates in the same way as you did the saucers, although you may prefer to make them oval in shape. Set the plates on the table, also.

Mould the largest ball of paste into a teapot shape. Pull out a spout from the body of the paste. Form the lid from another piece of paste and place it on top of the pot. The handle can be made from a very small sausage of paste. Moisten it with a little water and attach it to the teapot. Place the pot on one of the plates already on the table.

Standard Lamp

1 Roll out some pale yellow icing and place it over an object suitable for moulding a miniature lampshade.

2 Allow the lampshade to dry for a few days in a bowl of cornflour.

3 Roll out some brown icing and cut out a circle for the base. Roll out a sausage and insert into it a long bamboo skewer that will give the stand some strength and support.

4 Also set these parts aside for a few days to dry.

5 Assemble the lamp, using a little royal icing to join the parts, then set it beside the couch.

See colour plate

on page 139

Dragon Cake

A cake in the shape of a dragon provides a wonderful table centrepiece. The strong, bold colours, plus the glitter of gold, add to the dramatic effect. It makes a celebratory cake for anyone born in the year of the dragon, be they male, female, young or old, and an intriguing cake for those who like something different.

The cake illustrated required two quantities of cake mixture (500 g butter) and approximately 3 kg of bought soft icing.

Dragon Cake

Beer Stein Cake

(see page 146)

Shaping the Cake

The method used for making the dragon depends on how long the final cake is to be. If a short cake is required, a single cake may suffice. If, on the other hand, a long dragon is desired, several cakes may be baked in nutloaf tins, trimmed to the correct shape, then linked with icing. Alternatively, cakes may be baked in shaped foil trays. The cake seen in the colour plate was made from one cake baked in foil. However, when the dragon is for a party, it is prudent to make it from two cakes to provide more serves, so the following instructions are for a dragon using two cakes.

The decorating instructions given in this chapter are for covering fruit cakes. However, if only a single layer of icing is used and the fiery collar is omitted, it is possible to use any other firm cake recipe.

1 Press out the folded edges of two large foil trays. To make the first mould, cut away a triangular piece of foil from two diagonally opposite corners. Pull up the cut sides and mould the foil into a canoe-like shape, gently bending the middle section. Firmly fold the two ends of the canoe so that the cake mixture cannot escape during cooking. Repeat the procedure for the second tray.

2 When baking your cakes in foil trays do not forget to place a tray under them to catch any drips. Use two nutloaf tins if you prefer.

3 Once the cakes have cooled, cut away the surrounding foil or release them from the nutloaf tins. If nutloaf tins were used, the ends of the cakes will need to be trimmed a little; the cakes will also require a build up of icing at the middle on one side to create a boomerang shape.

Use some bought almond icing to fill in any holes around the tops and sides of the cakes.

4 Prepare a suitable presentation board for the dragon. The board in the illustration measured 75 cm by 35 cm. The board you choose needs to be thick enough to support the weight of the cakes, plus that of the icing, without bending and thereby cracking the dragon and its icing. A thick piece of laminated board is ideal. The sides of the board may be covered with ribbon or a decorative paper edging.

5 Scrape some royal icing (see Recipes chapter) on the base of the two cakes. So position them on the board that they begin to take on the shape of a dragon's body. Allow space for icing to be built up at the join of the two cakes and also at one end for the head, which is made completely from soft icing.

6 Using plenty of bought almond or soft icing, join the cakes harmoniously. Form a head from soft icing and connect it to the body. The head should be longer than it is wide. Give the icing curves and depressions to help create the impression of a dragon's head. Form two ears, and two large, upright scales on the forehead, the first between the ears and the second behind the first. Shape empty eye sockets and a raised, central ridge running down the face to the mouth. Form depressions for the nostrils and mouth. The dragon in the illustration also has bags under the eyes.

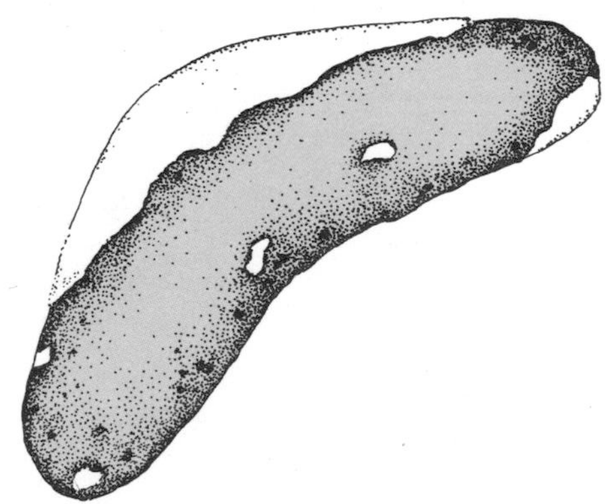

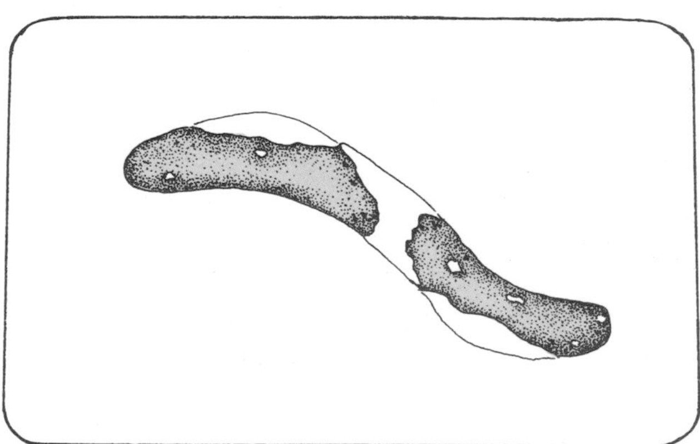

7 Shape a tail from soft icing and connect it to the cake, merging the icings of both sections.

Covering the Cake

1 Glaze the whole, except the head, with some warmed apricot jam. Roll out some almond icing and cover the glazed areas. The icing edge that meets the head needs to be pressed and stroked to ensure a smooth transition. See the chapter Covering the Cake for general instructions.

2 When the covering is complete, set the cake aside for a week to allow it to become firm.

3 Colour some soft icing grey or another suitable colour. Be sure to colour plenty of icing because the wings and legs will need to be moulded from this icing, and it is often difficult to duplicate a colour.

4 Glaze the whole cake, including the head, with egg white. The final covering is done in two sections and the join or seam needs to be pressed and smoothed to ensure its line disappears.

Roll out enough soft icing to cover the dragon's body, then apply it to the cake. Refer to the chapter on Covering the Cake again. Roll out some more icing and cover the head. Mould the icing so that the features already pressed into the head retain their shape. The ridges on the snout, the mouth, the nostrils and the spikes of the head all need to be seen. Use the colour plate or photographs of your favourite dragon to assist you.

5 Once all is complete, set the cake aside for several days or a week until it has dried thoroughly.

6 When the icing is firm enough to retain its tail shape, use the rounded end of a cutter (see the chapter on Equipment) to make a pattern of scales in it. The pattern may be worked over the entire body as well as at the end of the tail; allow it to fade away as you work towards the front of the dragon.

Completing the Details

Wings

1 Use more grey icing to make a pair of wings. The following pattern, which is drawn to scale for the dragon in the illustration, can be used as a guide. The wings are quite heavy and thick to enable them to stand upright on the dragon and remain curved. Roll out the icing to a thickness of 5–8 mm, then cut out a pair.

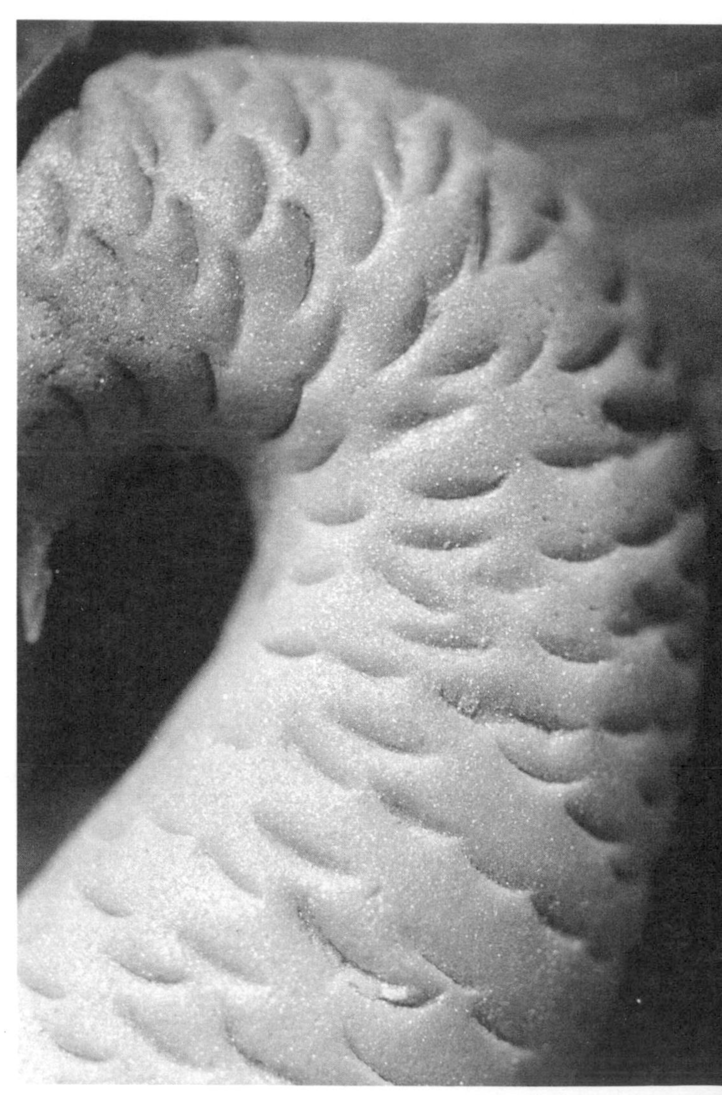

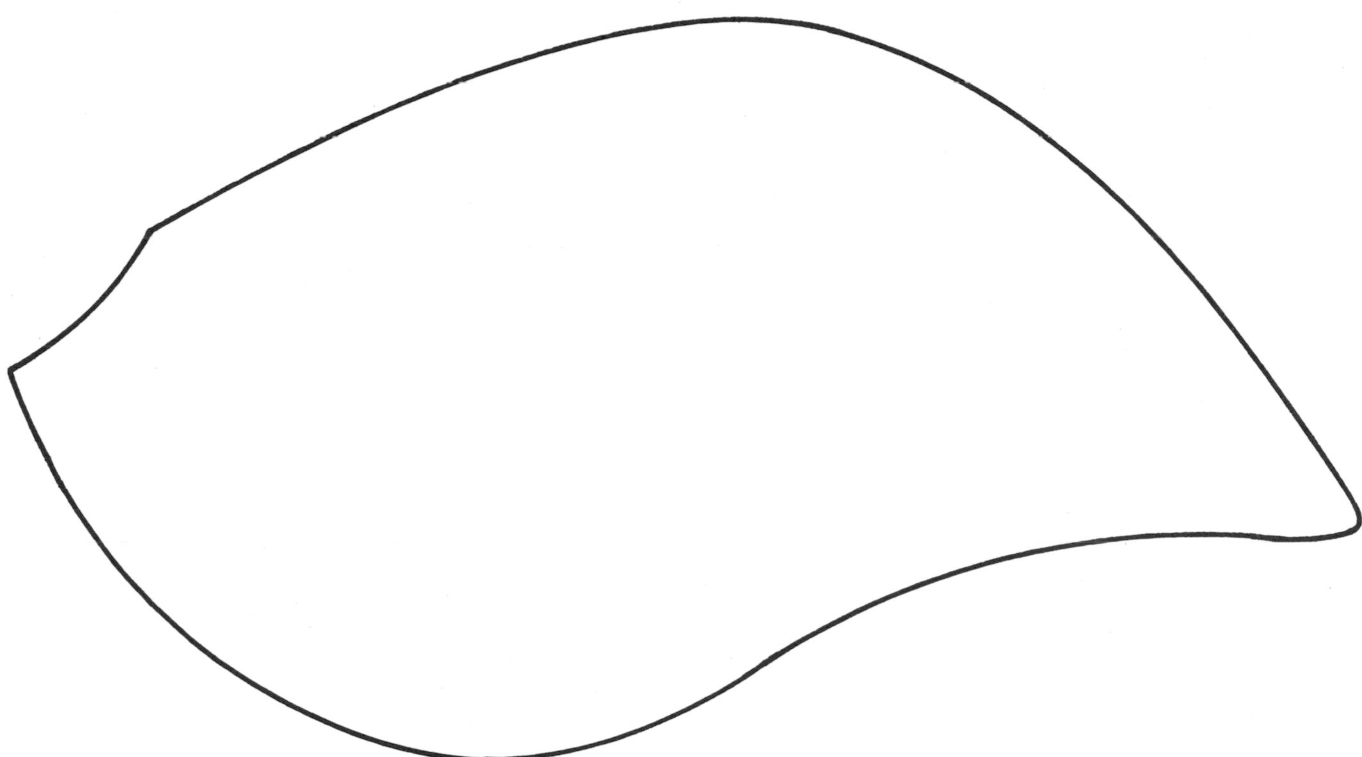

2 Frill the edges lightly to help make them finer. Do this by rolling the handle of a paintbrush along just the edges of the wings. Work back and forth, moving the icing all the time until all the edges have been worked. Use a little cornflour if the icing sticks to the handle. Cut a series of small incisions in the icing along the edges.

3 Give the wings veins, using a tool (see the chapter on Equipment). The markings can be made on both sides or just on the outsides of the wings.

4 Decide where you want to place the wings on the back of the dragon. Insert two short bamboo skewers in the back for each wing. Also insert two skewers into the base of each wing. As well, make two holes in the base of each wing – the skewers already placed in the dragon's back are pushed into these.

5 Moisten the base of one wing, hold it upright over the two skewers on one side of the dragon's back, then push it down onto them. Add the second wing in the same way. The two skewers in each wing will need to be pushed through the icing into the dragon's back. Hold the wings at the base while you are placing them in position to give them some support and to reduce the risk of breakage. Smooth the join of wings and back by pressing the icing with your fingers.

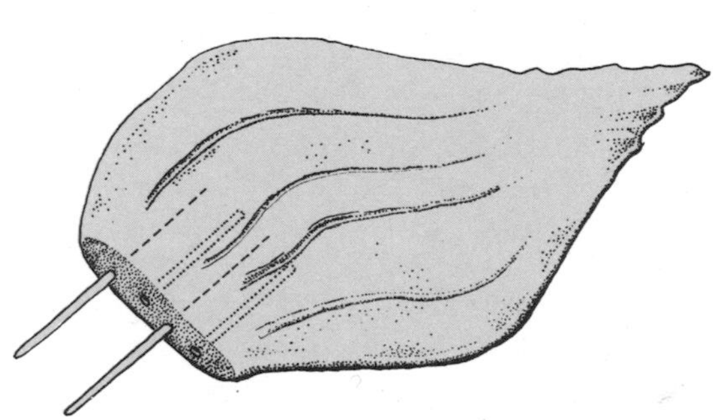

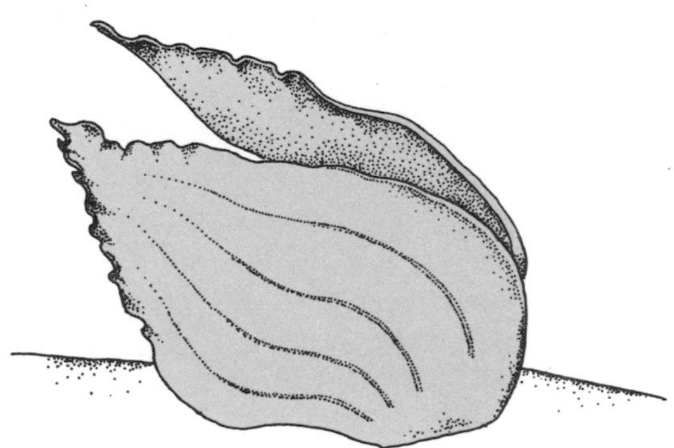

Legs

1 Divide some grey icing into two equal parts. Roll both into stubby cones. Using a pair of scissors, make two 2-cm-length incisions at the thin end of both cones. Press and mould the cut sections to form three-clawed dragon's feet. Each claw will have a red nail at its tip, so ensure that the ends of the claws are flat and smooth.

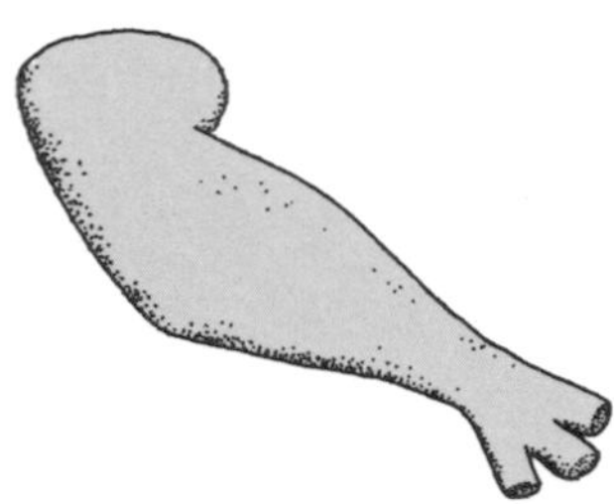

2 Press and mould the tops of both legs, making sure that the surfaces that will meet the body are flat. Moisten these surfaces, then place one leg on each side of the dragon's body. Press and smooth the joins to ensure the limbs are well attached. If you are concerned about the limbs adhering, insert one or two skewers in them before they are attached. Bend and curve the legs.

3 Use the rounded end of a small cutter to make a pattern of scales on the surface of each leg. Make a series of lines along the length of each claw.

Set the dragon aside for a few days to allow the wings and legs to dry.

Red Trimmings

The dragon in the colour plate has been given many red spikes and a red tip to its tail. It also has frilled and curled pieces attached to it, representing flames. These are quite large around the neck, but as they descend towards the tail they become smaller and smaller. Use the patterns provided as a guide, although it is not essential to recreate them precisely.

1 Take some soft icing and colour it a bright, fiery red. A combination of red and yellow powdered food colouring achieves the best results.

2 Roll out some red icing and cut from it two small strips of icing 5 cm long and 1–2 cm wide. Cut a zig-zag effect along one long side of both strips, then frill it with the handle of a paintbrush. Moisten the back of the other long sides of both strips and place them against the body where the two legs join. See the colour plate for further assistance.

3 Make a number of spikes to place on the dragon's back and tail. Mould pieces of red soft icing into triangles with your hands. Make the spikes in graded sizes. Moisten the bases of the triangles and press them into place.

Five small spikes are placed at the tip of the tail and another, graded, five are placed further up, at the wider part of the tail. Seven large, graded spikes commence on the back, a little to the front of the wings, and progress to the second grey spike on the head. There are also extra, small spikes located at the beginning of many of the red, frilled flames.

4 Roll out more red icing and, using the patterns provided, cut out a number of flames. The larger pattern is for the flames around the dragon's neck and face. Use the handle of a paintbrush to frill all the edges so that they become very thin and curled. Moisten the backs of the top sections of the shapes with a little water, then attach the flames, using the colour plate as a guide.

The flames are attached near and along the spikes of the body and tail. A rich layer of large frills is placed around the head like a collar, while smaller flames are added to the sides of the face and nostrils.

Complete the face by placing three small, red spikes on the centre ridge between the eyes, as shown in the colour plate.

5 Make six red nails for the claws. Moisten the edges that will join the claws, then attach the nails.

Tail

Shape a small, red tail tip and merge it with the end of the tail. Curve the tip to make it look realistic.

Eyes

1 Use a combination of white- and black-coloured soft icing to make the eyes, varying the colour, and perhaps even adding a small amount of red icing, to suggest glints. The eyes need to fit snugly into the eye sockets that have already been moulded in the head.

2 When you are happy with the shape and size of the eyes, moisten the backs of the eyes and insert them in place. Use a pottery tool to press them into a realistic shape. Use the colour plate as a reference.

Colouring

Once the dragon is complete, give parts of the body, legs, face and wings a light frosting of gold petal dust to create the typical appearance of reptile skin. Use red petal dust to highlight the red on the dragon and black petal dust to give some of the spikes and flames just a touch of darkness at their tips.

Set the dragon aside until required. Decorate the sides of the board with red ribbon or gold paper tape, attached with PVC glue.

See colour plate

on page 140

Beer Stein Cake

The Beer Stein Cake is a classic cake that will appeal to many men. Whether you are celebrating a birthday, Father's Day or a promotion, this is a suitable cake. However, it is best for smaller rather than large gatherings.

Although the Beer Stein Cake shown in the colour plate is blue, many other colours are suitable. The decorative features can be applied either in white or a paler shade of the tone used for the covering. The decorative features of the cake illustrated do demand some artistry, skill and confidence on the part of the decorator. However, you can copy the simpler floral or scroll patterns found on some steins and still achieve a striking cake.

For best results use a fruit cake or a nutloaf recipe (see Recipes chapter), because these are firmer and easier to work with than other recipes. Bought almond and soft icings should be employed for the covering because they provide the best base for the style of decoration used on this cake.

The cake illustrated used half a quantity of basic fruit cake mixture (125 g butter) and 800 g of soft icing.

Shaping the Cake

1 Bake the cake in a small nutloaf tin or a similar round tin. Note that the cake needs to be squat rather than high, though not too wide, otherwise the stein will look cumbersome.

2 Once the cake is cool remove it from the tin. An initial build-up of almond icing is added to help achieve the stein effect. This icing is applied to the sides of the round cake: thickly at the base and very thinly near the top to give the stein its characteristic tapering look.

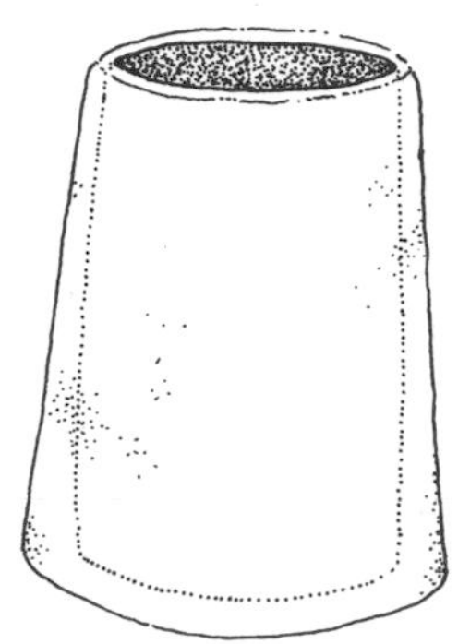

Covering the Cake

1 Use almond icing to fill any holes or dents in the cake surface that remains uncovered. Glaze all surfaces, except the base, with a little warmed apricot jam. Roll out some almond icing to a rectangle that is thick along one length and thin along the other. The measurements of the rectangle should be those of the cake's height by circumference.

2 Place the cake on its side at one end of the rectangle. Roll the cake along the length of the icing until the icing completely surrounds the cake. Press along the side join, rubbing gently until the seam disappears.

3 Roll out some more almond icing. Cut out a small circle and place it on top of the cake. Press around the circle's edge to merge the top with the sides.

4 Allow the cake to dry for a few days.

5 Colour about 750 g of soft icing for the second covering, making sure you prepare enough icing for a lid and handle as well. Cover the cake in the same way that you did for the first covering.

6 Set the cake aside to dry for a few more days.

7 Attach the cake to a small presentation board by scraping a little royal icing onto the board, then pressing the cake down into place.

Lid and Rims

Lid

1 On a board, roll some of the remaining coloured soft icing into a ball with your hands, then continue to roll it until the base spreads and a shallow mound is formed. Use a small rolling-pin to flatten out the edge of the mound until a suitably sized lid is achieved.

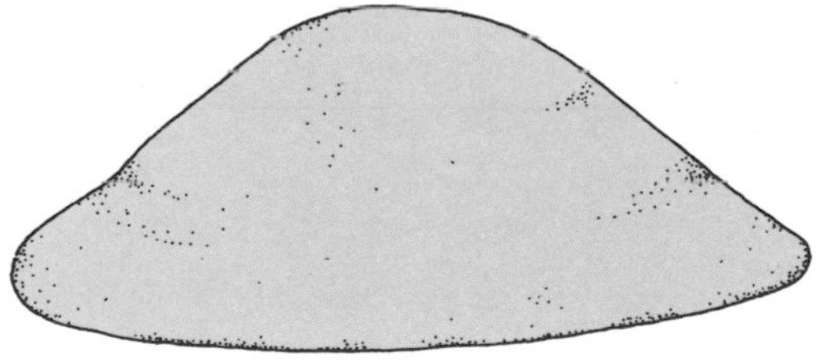

2 Smooth the edge of the lid, then use a suitable leatherwork tool or an engraved button or teaspoon to make a pattern in the icing around the circumference. Repeat the pattern in ascending circles. Finally, form a suitable knob from the very top icing of the lid. (If this breaks off, don't worry – just attach it to the top of the lid again.)

3 When the lid is completed, place it on a piece of waxed paper and set it aside to dry for a few days.

4 As soon as the top of the lid appears to be firm, fill a bowl with cornflour and place the lid upside down in it. This will ensure that the lid dries evenly, so that its base does not distort when it is placed on the stein.

5 Once both the cake and the lid are completely dry assemble the stein. Place a small quantity of royal icing on the top of the cake, then place the lid in position.

Top and Base Rims

1 Roll some leftover coloured soft icing into a short sausage. The sausage needs to be as long as the circumference of the stein's base. Moisten around the base of the cake with a little water, then place the sausage in position. Using either a finger or a suitable tool, press the sausage between the cake and the board. The rim must look concave. Trim away any excess icing, then moisten and join the two ends. Press and smooth the icing of the rim until it is as even as possible.

2 Make another sausage from some more coloured soft icing. Moisten the cake just below the lid, add the sausage and cut away any excess icing. Press the sausage to create the same concave effect you achieved for the rim at the base. Once again trim away any excess icing.

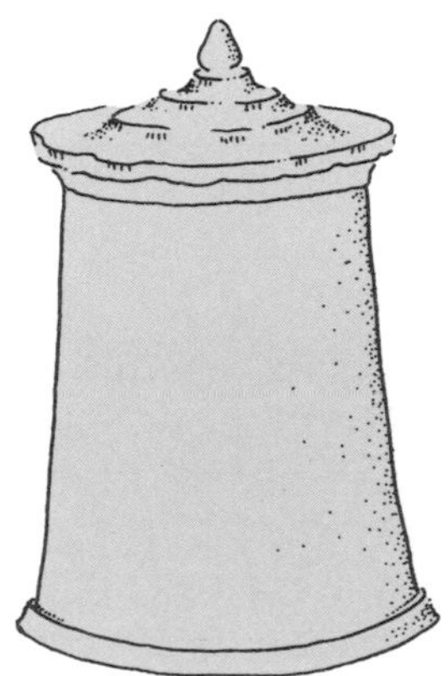

3 Set the cake aside to dry for several days.

Stein Decorations

The decorations on the stein shown in the colour plate have all been created with a white soft icing. The design, which is done freehand, involves a scene that flows around the cake, with no section repeated. It offers you a starting point, a scene that you can easily adapt to meet your particular needs.

1 Roll out a very small quantity of white soft icing as thinly as possible. Moisten one side of the icing and place it on the lower part of the cake to form part of the foreground. Using your fingers, press the icing outwards. This will thin

the icing further and also spread it over a larger area.

Cut out some small triangles of icing and moisten them on one side. Place them on the cake so that they appear to be trees on the skyline.

Continue in this way until there is a foreground around half of the cake and trees appear at intermittent intervals across it.

Use some more icing to create clouds and cut out some small house shapes. Apply these in the same way as you did the trees.

2 Once all shapes have been applied to the surface of the first half, use suitable tools and skewers to engrave lines, creases, folds and ridges in the white icing to suggest: the features of the landscape; the roof, windows and door of the house; and the texture and foliage of the trees. Where necessary, add more icing to represent slopes and rocks in the foreground and hills in the distance, so that the scene takes on a three-dimensional appearance.

3 Decorate the second half of the cake, using the same techniques. Allow the design to merge with the scene of the first half where they meet.

If the river, bridge and horse and cart illustrated are to be included in your scene leave a space in the middle of the second half for them, when you are adding other features. Once again use tools to engrave details on the white icing.

Stein Handle

1 Roll some of the coloured icing into a sausage about 1 cm in diameter. Push several strands of wire through its length. Bend and curve the wire-encased icing to form a handle, then trim the icing and the wires: the icing should be the proper handle length, but the wires should protrude by 1.5 cm at each end.

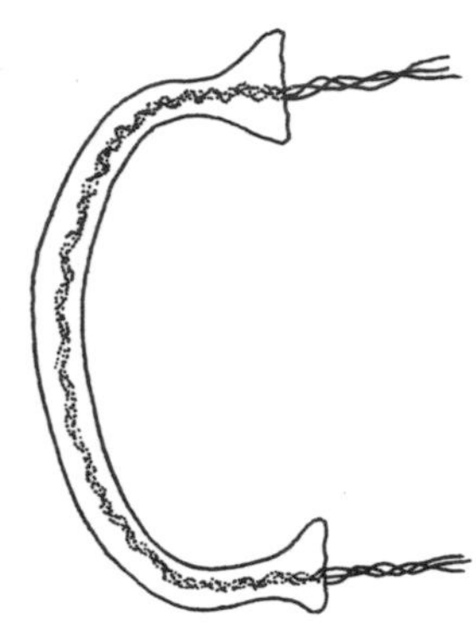

2 Make holes in the cake, with a skewer, near the top and base of the cake where the handle will go, and moisten around them. Attach the handle by pushing the wires through the holes. Gently press around the joins.

Cotton wool placed under and to either side of the handle can be used as a support until the handle is dry.

3 Make the part of the handle that attaches to the stein lid from another piece of wire-encased

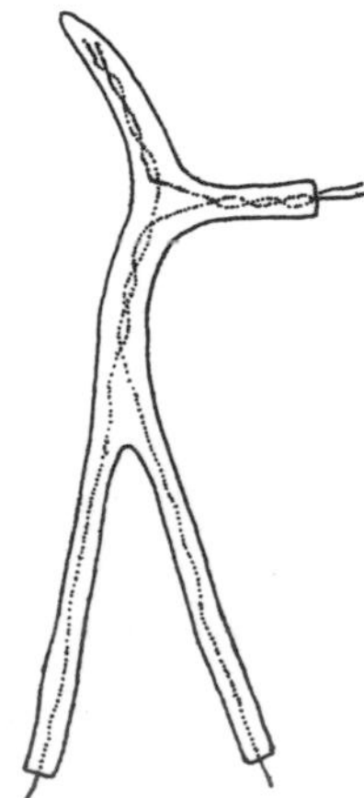

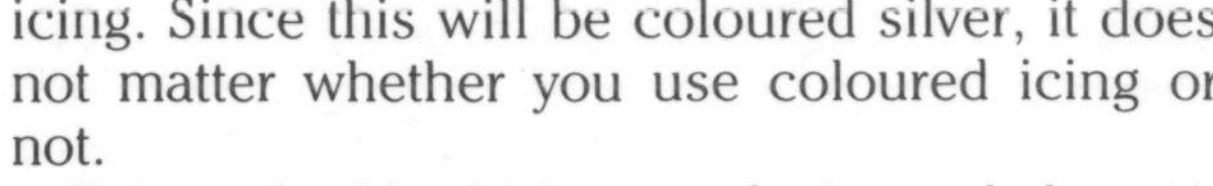
icing. Since this will be coloured silver, it does not matter whether you use coloured icing or not.

Take a double thickness of wire and shape it to a 't'. Ensure the shape is long enough to go from the lid to the handle and that it divides in two at the end that will wrap around the handle.

4 Wrap icing around the wire, ensuring it is completely covered. The top of the 't' piece should be somewhat broad and flat to represent a thumb-rest.

5 While the icing is still soft and pliable, insert the right-angle section of the 't' in the lid and wrap the two base ends around the handle of the stein. Press and squeeze the icing of these ends so that they join underneath the top of the stein handle.

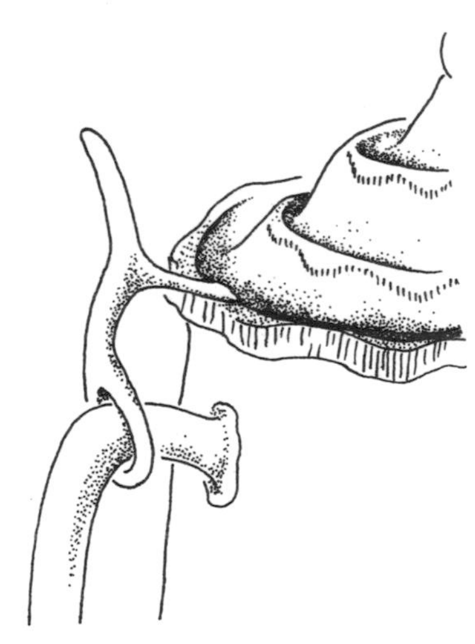

6 Allow the lid handle to dry thoroughly before colouring it silver.

Silver Colouring

Use the colour plate as a guide to the parts of the stein that are coloured silver. The parts are coloured by brushing on silver powder mixed with methylated spirits. A little dry silver powder can also be brushed lightly on the very outer edge of the lid, if a frosted appearance is required.

See colour plate

on page 110

Banksia Cones

The delightful Banksia Cones can be made just as sugar sculptures or, if preferred, from small, oval-shaped cakes. Any cake recipe is suitable. When using cakes, you need cover them with one layer of coloured soft icing only.

The cones represent banksias at both the flowering and the seed stages. The flowering sections have been made by using several large, yellow stamens.

A child's birthday cake can be made up of a number of cones, assembled on a large presentation board, so that each guest can receive a whole small cake. For the marzipan enthusiast offer a gift comprising two cones decorated in coloured marzipan instead of soft icing.

The cones illustrated require a quarter of a quantity of cake mixture (60 g butter) or 500 g of bought marzipan for the shapes. If cakes are used, 500 g of bought soft icing is also required for covering the shapes. Approximately 100 g of marzipan or soft icing is needed for the decoration.

Shaping the Cones

Using Cakes

1 Make two small, oval-shaped cake pans, using heavy-duty aluminium foil. Cut the foil into two 20-cm squares, then fold each diagonally to create canoe-like moulds. Fold them two or three times at both ends, so that they hold together firmly. Curve both sides of each and flatten the bases of both so that the cake mixture will not run out during baking. Trim away any excess foil.

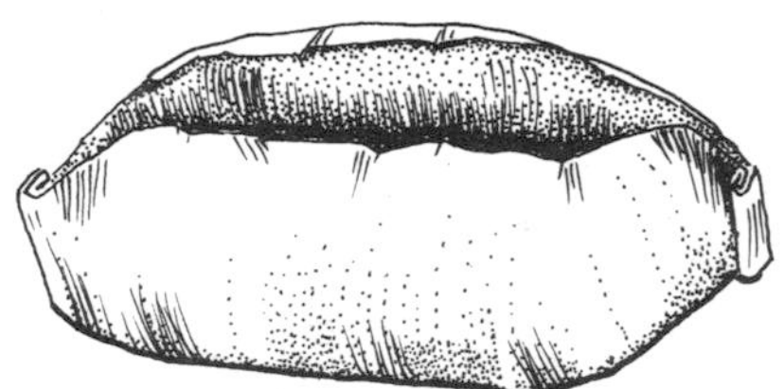

2 Choose any cake mixture from the Recipes chapter. When the cakes are cool, remove the foil around them and place them on a small, oval, foil-covered presentation board, first scraping a little royal icing (see Recipes chapter) on their bases to ensure they stay in place.

3 Cover the cakes with soft icing coloured dark brown, following the instructions given in the chapter on Covering the Cake.

4 Make soft icing or marzipan stems for both. Mark the icing in the way described in Step 3 of Using Marzipan (below).

Using Marzipan

1 Colour 500 g of marzipan deep brown. Use 2–5 drops of brown food colouring or a pinch of brown powdered food colouring, adding more if the icing does not become dark enough. Knead the icing very well, then divide it in two.

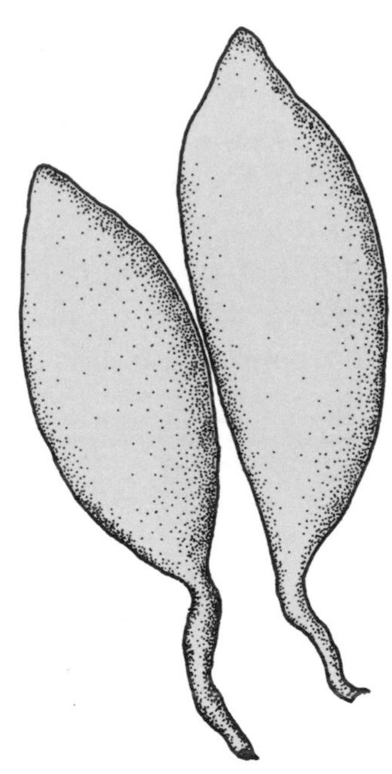

2 Shape the marzipan into two oval cones, allowing a little for the stems. The cones in the colour plate measure approximately 15 cm in length, 6 cm in width and 4 cm in height from the board. Shape their tops to a curved point. Their bases will require 3–5-cm-long stems. For the best visual effect make one cone slightly larger than the other.

Place the cones on a presentation board, making sure you scrape a little royal icing on their undersides so that they remain in place.

3 Make indentations in the top and bottom sections of the cones, using the rounded base of any small cutter (see the Equipment chapter).

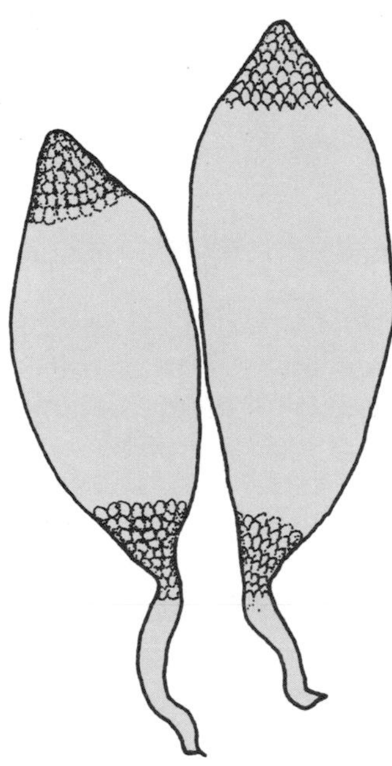

Decorating the Cones

Seed Pockets

1 To make the opened seed pockets, begin by colouring a small amount of soft icing or marzipan pale brown. Press some of the previously coloured dark icing with your fingers to form a circle about 2 cm in diameter. Moisten one side of this and then at its centre flatten a small ball of light brown icing. Ensure a small rim of darker icing can be seen around the light brown. Fold the piece in half, with the light icing on the inside, and moisten the fold on the outside. Press the piece onto one cone. Repeat the procedure several times until four pieces have been placed on the smaller cone and eight on the larger one. Use the colour plate as a guide.

2 Make a number of unopened seed pockets from the dark icing and place six on the small cone and three on the larger. The pockets are made by shaping some icing into small, pastie-like shapes. They are placed on the cone with their curved part facing up.

Dead Stamens

1 Next the spent flower stamens that have grown old and mat the surface of the cones are made. Make a quantity of soft-peak royal icing (see Recipes chapter) and colour it very dark brown. Use either dark brown powdered food colouring or several tablespoonsful of cocoa. Mix very well to ensure the icing is smooth and lump-free. The icing may also need to be a little softer than usual, because it has to be free flowing. Use a little lemon juice to soften it, if necessary.

2 Make a paper-cone bag (see Equipment chapter), fit it with a number 00 writing tube and fill it with the brown icing. Pipe numerous squiggles over much of the two cones. Use the colour plate as a guide. The smaller cone has squiggles piped from below its yellow stamens to its base, just above the stem. The larger cone has dead and hardened stamens piped from 2 cm below its tip to a little above its stem. Note that there are no piped squiggles on the seed pockets.

3 Make some white soft-peak royal icing and, using a paper-cone bag and number 00 writing tube, pipe just a few strands over the top of some of the dark brown squiggles, as shown in the colour plate.

Banksia Babies

1 Colour small amounts of soft icing or marzipan for the heads of the banksia babies red,

brown and orange. Make ten small balls from the orange icing to represent faces. Place small balls of white soft icing or marzipan on them for eyes. Use a little brown icing to make the hats and place some on the white eyes, also. Use very tiny pieces of red icing to make the mouths. Cut some yellow stamens to lengths of about 1 cm and insert several into the points of the hats.

2 Moisten the back of the completed faces and insert them into some of the open seed pockets.

Stamens

Only the smaller cone has stamens. The stamens commence close to the top of the cone and finish at the beginning of the piped, dead stamen squiggles.

1 Cut a number of large, yellow stamens to about 1 cm in length.

2 The top of the section is decorated with the curled cottons of the stamens only, to represent the unopened spikes. The curled cottons are placed in rows across the width of the cone.

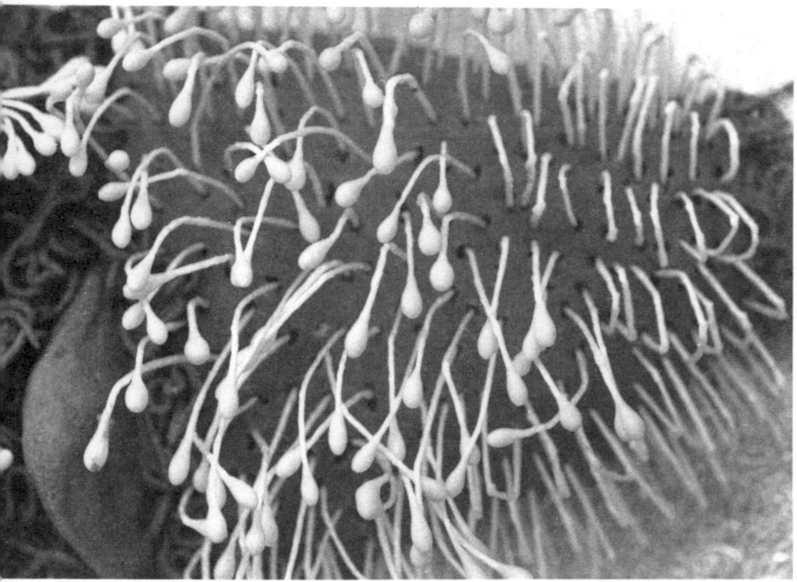

3 Once several rows of curled cottons have been put in place, add stamens to the smaller cone in descending rows, increasing their lengths as they come closer to the piped squiggles. Be sure to bend the stamens to give them a realistic appearance.

Leaves

Five leaves make up the final decoration on the cones.

1 Colour a small amount of soft icing or marzipan pale green. Roll it out to a long, thin piece from which cut five long pieces, 1.5–2.5 cm in width. Using a pair of scissors, give the five pieces serrated edges.

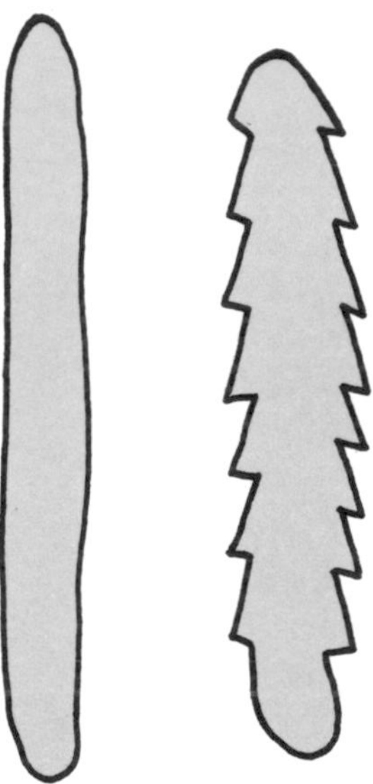

2 Cut the top and bottom of the five pieces to softly pointed ends, then make a long, central, indented vein in the icing, for the length of each leaf. Use the handle of a paintbrush to flute the edges of all the leaves. Place the handle on the very edge of each leaf and roll it back and forward. Move the leaf until every section of its edge has been worked. This action softens the edges of the leaves and make them look more realistic.

3 Moisten the backs of the leaves in a few places, then drape them softly over the stems and the board. Use the colour plate as a guide.

Index

Page numbers in *italics* refer to colour plates.